MONARCHY as DEMOCRACY

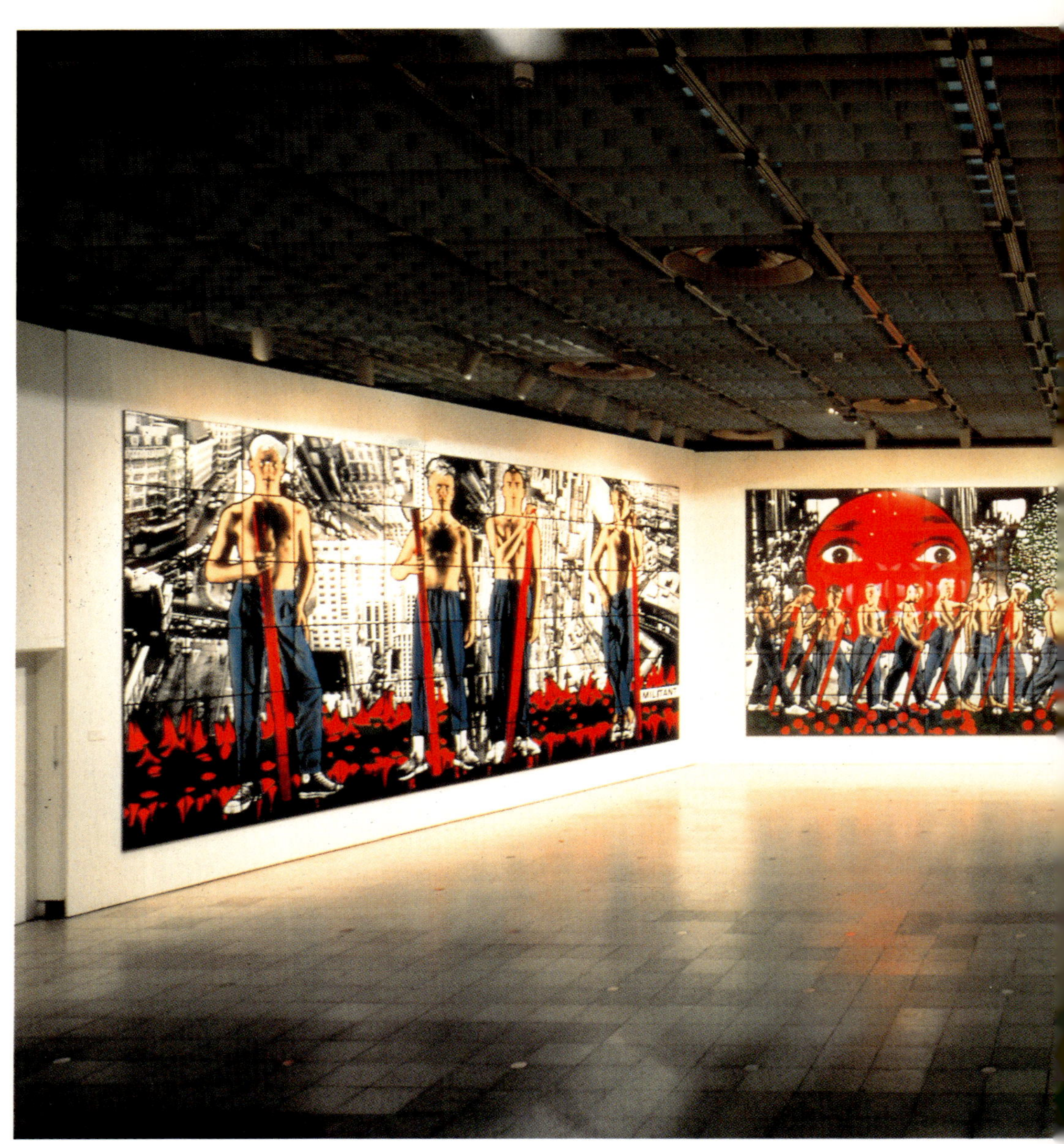

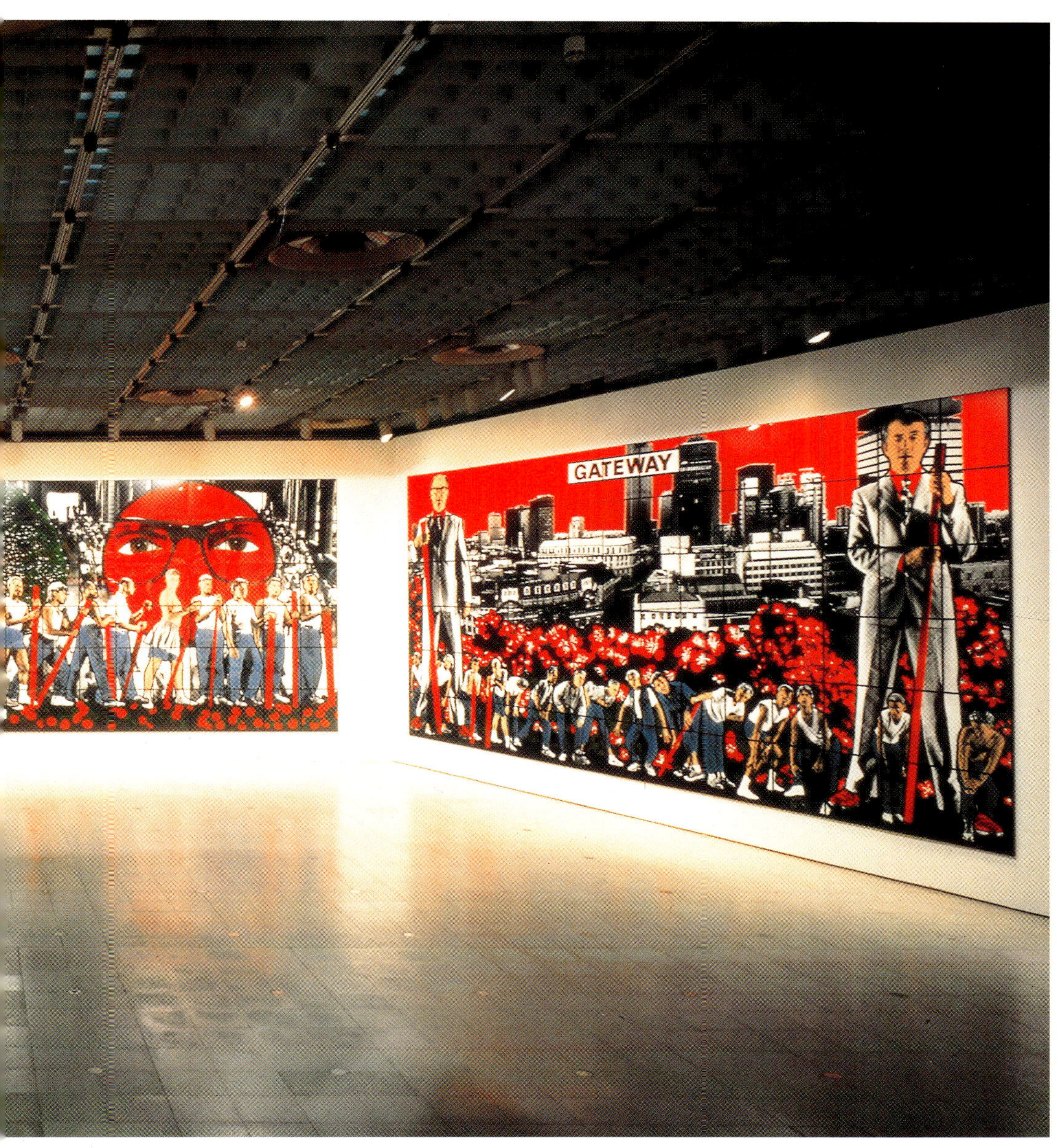
GATEWAY

Wolf Jahn

on the Tryptych

CLASS WAR   MILITANT   GATEWAY

by

GILBERT & GEORGE

Anthony d'Offay Gallery
London 1991

Cover: Detail of CLASS WAR

Frontispiece CLASS WAR   MILITANT   GATEWAY
in the exhibition PICTURES 1982 TO 1986,
Hayward Gallery, London, 1987

Translation: David Britt
Produced in Germany by Uwe Kraus GmbH, Murr
ISBN 0-947564-37-3

CONTENTS

LOOKING IN

THE HISTORICAL CLASS STRUGGLE

The history of all hitherto existing society is the history of class struggles. Freeman and slave, patrician and plebeian, lord and serf, guild-master and journeyman, in a word, oppressor and oppressed, stood in constant opposition to one another, carried on an uninterrupted, now hidden, now open fight, a fight that each time ended, either in a revolutionary reconstitution of society at large, or in the common ruin of the contending classes.[1]

It is more than a hundred years since Karl Marx and Friedrich Engels wrote these words and thus gave the Manifesto of the Communist Party its historical dimension. Looking forward in hope to a future society that would be classless, because Communist, they identified conflict between classes as a consistent feature of all past societies. In their own time, the authors of the Manifesto regarded these warring classes – the oppressors and the oppressed – as having been reduced to just two parties, the bourgeoisie and the proletariat:

> Our epoch, the epoch of the bourgeoisie, possesses, however, this distinctive feature: it has simplified the class antagonisms. Society as a whole is more and more splitting up into two great hostile camps, into two great classes directly facing each other: Bourgeoisie and Proletariat.[2]

Seen in this historical perspective, the task for the future was clear: the abolition of the bourgeoisie and the rule of the proletariat. The classes were to disappear and make way for a single class; and that class would be the proletariat. This served to predefine the political actions that would ultimately eliminate the universal class struggle – a term coined by Marx and Engels – and institute a classless society in which former antagonisms would for ever be reconciled. The collective life of human beings would thenceforth involve neither oppressors nor oppressed, neither exploiters nor exploited. The future belonged to a peaceable society in which every individual would find his own happiness in his own way.

Subsequent history has shown the extent to which that utopian vision of a classless society has come true. In different ways, the democratization of many hitherto hierarchical structures of power, and the establishment of Communist states, are both efforts to pursue the utopia of the classless state. But opinions differ widely as to the degree of its realization. The present situation is marked by widely varying assessments of what has been achieved, of what remains to be achieved, and of the status quo itself. Some see the Western democracies as a covert form of authoritarian state, in which an economic system has assumed the role of oppressor; others find in the countries under Communist rule the suppression of personal freedom in all its forms.

Divergent assessments aside, however, one increasingly apparent phenomenon is the disappearance of the political will historically defined by the term class war. Class war seems, indeed, to be abolishing itself. This is primarily a result of the economic factor by which it has all along been governed. The proletariat formerly defined itself as the class of the exploited, as it carried out productive work for the benefit of its oppressors; but in the age of the third industrial revolution such a definition is becoming increasingly suspect. More and more, machines, robots, and advanced electronics are taking over the work that was formerly done by human hands and in the sweat of the human brow. The utopian vision of a machine-shop empty of human beings has long since become a reality. Industry, the locus of productive work, has gone the same way as agriculture. The latter now offers employment only to a small number of individuals; and the same is already starting to happen in industrial production. Technology is replacing human labour.

This fact – the replacement of the "exploited" class by modern techniques of manufacture – makes the historical class war irrelevant. Where exploitation no longer exists, the struggle of the oppressed against their oppressors makes no sense. But whether this leads to a classless utopia, and consequently to individual fulfilment for all, seems more than dubious. True, the oppressors are less oppressive – in Marx's and Engel's sense – than before; but the former victims of oppression are still a long way from using their new-found "freedom" to attain true self-determination and democratic fellowship. And what are they? Democratized but still unfree masses? The unemployed, the would-be workers, the new poor?

In the light of all these developments, it is disconcerting to find Gilbert & George, in 1986, reverting in one of their works to the theme of class war; it was in the following year that they presented the work to the public for the first time (p. 2/3). Disconcerting, because, things being as they are, the class war plays rather a marginal part in current politics. In place of the need to overcome class antagonisms, the political debate tends to concentrate on such themes as environmental pollution, ecology, disarmament negotiations, nuclear technology, détente between West and East, and the bridging of the econonomic gulf between North and South. Not much is heard of the class war, and that is mostly in circles that exist, from the state's point of view, on the outer limits of legality. Those isolated radical groupings that still define their political aims in class war terms have started to look more like the remnants of a formerly coherent, Communist-minded resistance front than like the mouthpieces of a broadly based movement. Furthermore, the Communist states themselves are in the midst of the most serious crisis in their history: they show signs of disintegration and decay, with a constant hollowing out from within. Communism seems to be in retreat. Class war slogans hold very little conviction; they convey only the obtuse defiance of doomed functionaries, on whose lips the phrase "class war" sounds more like an abdication than an incitement to revolt.

There is every reason to ask, therefore, why artists should choose to present so weighty a theme as class war at a time when it is manifestly disappearing from view. Are they trying to reactivate it, to reflect it, to remodel it, or to present themselves as its critics? Or is this a pictorial parody, a cynical aside on the high-flown rhetoric of class war? Such questions find their justification in the external form of the picture itself. CLASS WAR (p. 12/13) forms the dominant central panel of a triptych more than 25 metres long, the wings of which are GATEWAY (p. 26/27) and MILITANT (p. 30/31). Gilbert & George have thus adopted a pictorial typ derived from the altarpiece: a form of presentation designed in the first place to display a narrative of salvation. Does this triptych therefore embody such a narrative? And if so, why is this called CLASS WAR, flanked and supported both by a GATEWAY and by the epithet MILITANT? Answers to these questions will be supplied in the present essay. Piece by piece and image by image, it elucidates the triptych, so that by the end its meaning has been extracted and its political dimension revealed.

THE TRIPTYCH

Before separating the triptych into its several components, and then fitting these together again, it is necessary first to point to the fundamental affinities that unite the three pictures. Apart from their common height, they share a division into a foreground and a background, occupied in all

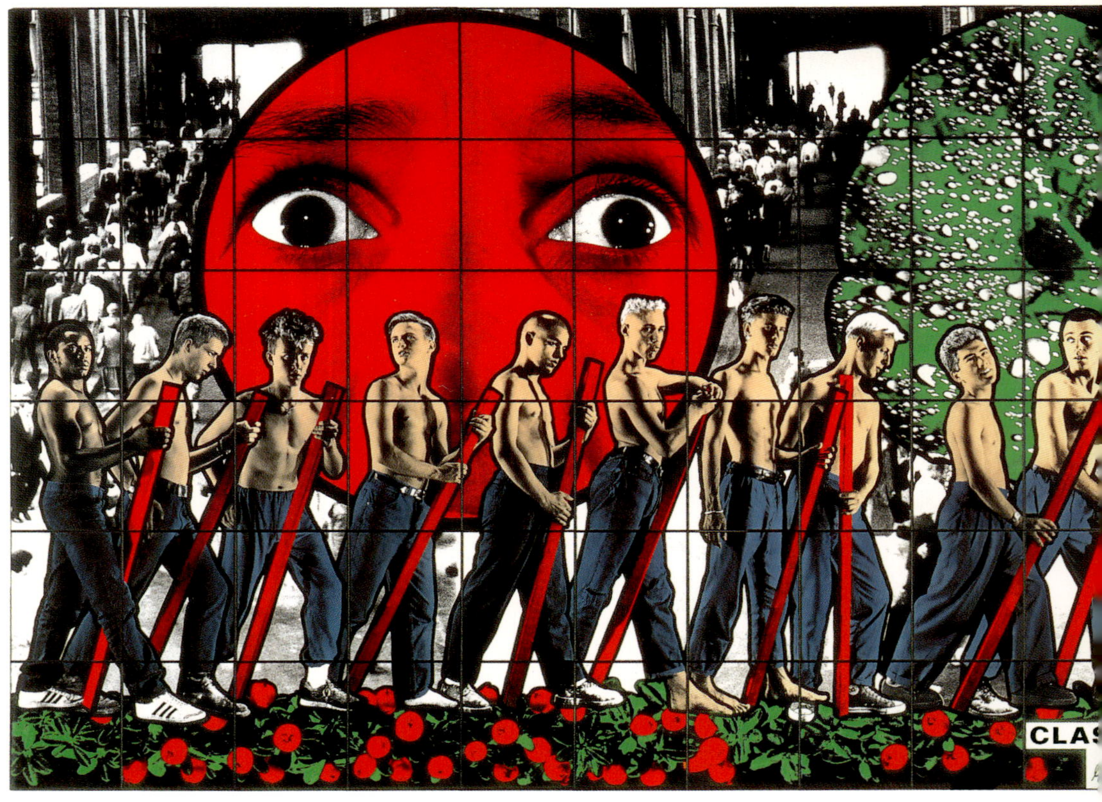

CLASS WAR from CLASS WAR, MILITANT, GATEWAY, 1986, 363 x 1010 cm.

three cases by similar, omnipresent motifs. These will serve as initial points of reference for this interpretation. The foreground in each case displays plant motifs, together with a line of young men with staves in their hands. In the background are urban scenes. The foreground is coloured; the background is largely black and white. The individual foreground motifs are handled separately and lit distinctively; those in the background are not, but are lit by natural light alone. These features signal to the viewer that the foreground is the scene of the central event whose motifs generate the action, and that the background supplies the spatial context for those active figures that appear before it. This account of the work accordingly begins in the foreground, before moving to find corroboration in the background.

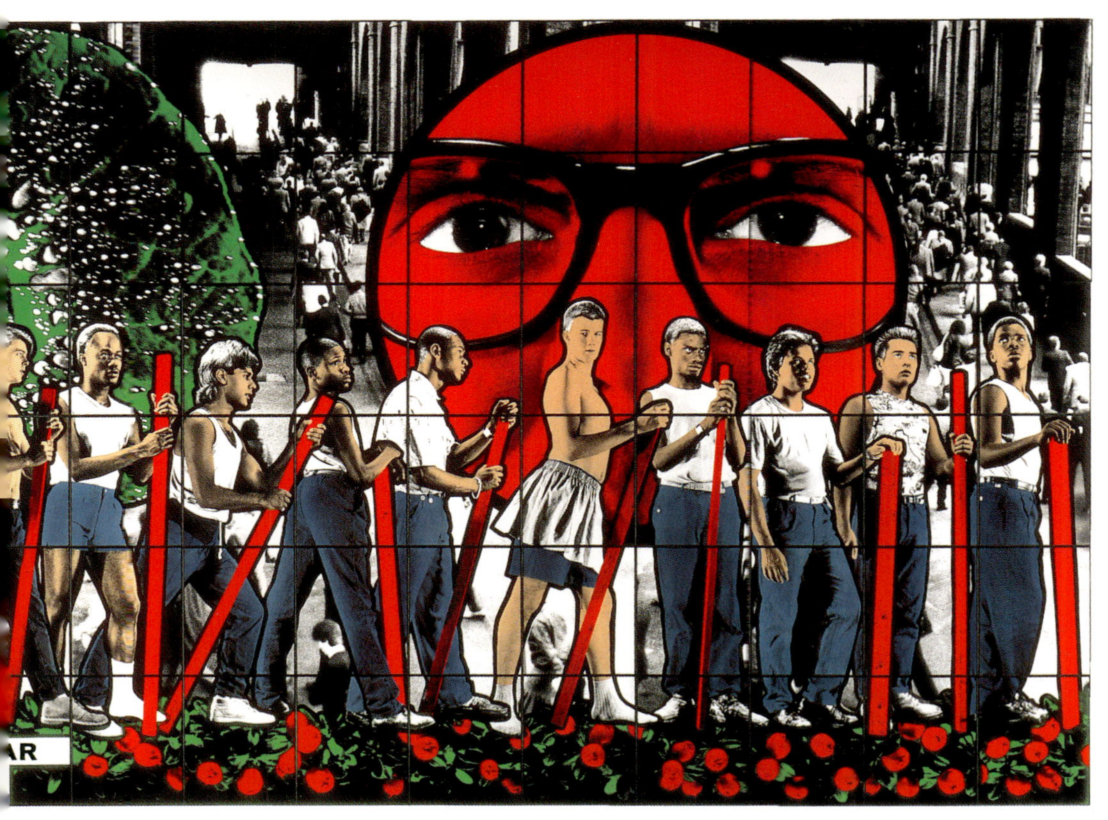

CLASS WAR

Across the whole width of the foreground of CLASS WAR (p. 12/13), the central and largest picture in the triptych, there marches a procession of human figures. This moves from left to right along a strip of foliage and berries. Its numerous members, all of them young men, hold staves in their hands on which they lean for support as they walk. They have in common their age, their direction of movement, and their sex; and the resultant impression of unity is reinforced by a unified colour scheme. All wear blue trousers, and all carry red staves.

Backing this procession are three large, prominent, circular motifs. To left and right two bright, wide-open pairs of human eyes stare out frontally at the viewer. The centre is dominated by a round nasturtium leaf; drops of water, distributed over its whole surface, endow it with a look of literally dewy freshness. The background, finally, takes up the processional theme of the foreground. Four paths, on which masses of humanity press on towards a light-filled gateway, mark a rhythmic repetition of the procession in the foreground. But while the latter is arranged horizontally, the paths in the background lead upwards from below. The contrast is not only one of colour and lighting but also of orientation.

LIGHT AND SHADE – THE PATH OF LIGHT

Besides the compositional division of CLASS WAR – marked by protagonists, other figures, directions of movement and circular motifs – a notable feature of the picture is the strongly dynamic lighting of the foreground procession. In spite of all the features that unite the participants, one small distinction divides the procession into two groups; and this is primarily a distinction of tone. At the beginning, in the right-hand half of the picture, the figures all wear a white upper garment; in the left-hand half, they walk with torsos bared. The procession is thus divided into two by a factor of colour, a distinction between light and dark; and this, together with the directional movement, makes it into a progression from one element into another, from darkness to lightness. As if to emphasize this progression, the background also pursues – four times over – the same movement towards the light. This aspect, easily overlooked at first sight, signals both the theme of CLASS WAR and that of the triptych as a whole. This movement of human beings from dark to light marks the starting-point, the dynamic, and the mainspring of class conflict. Gilbert & George use it to frame their perspective of a modern class war.

The impulse to pass from dark to light, the emergence from darkness into the light of liberty, initially looks like a commonplace. There are countless metaphors describing, over and over again, the laborious process of liberation from the prison walls of darkness into radiant realms of bliss. Whether in the proverbial image of the phoenix arising from its own ashes, or in the motto "Per aspera ad astra" – through hardship to the stars – or in light-related images like the "Sun State", the "Sun King" or the "Enlightenment", there is a strong tendency to glorify light as the goal and the consummation of human wishes.

This welter of related wish-fulfilment images tends to provoke a weary feeling of alienation. The further this one metaphor penetrates into every realm of ideas, serious or otherwise, the more it tends to lose its meaning. It might seem to have declined into a mere slogan, ineffectual and devoid of truth: a verbal husk, derived from ancient myth, but in its modern guise no more than a form of words. At best, its meaning seems to have dwindled to a mere decorative interplay of contrasts – day and night, above and below, Heaven and Hell – that are much employed but little understood.

To do justice to the interplay of dark and light values in CLASS WAR, it remains necessary to look briefly into its essential significance. For although the purifying path of ascent from darkness into light now looks to us – because it reaches us from the past – like a historical and at times an obsolete idea, it is actually ahistorical and unconnected with any specific cultural context. In its essence, this is an intercultural, a universal human motif. It has existed and still exists everywhere and in every age, in numerous variants, interpretations and forms. It is to be found in Africa as much as in Asia, in modern literature as much as in alchemy. Its images speak of a store of human experience that has a timeless and perennial existence, but which for that reason embraces time and history within itself. The path of light itself is an embodiment of space and time. It is directly tied to the insight that all life exists in the tension between life and death. Every living being – but also every age, every epoch and every new form of awareness – passes along this path.

The presence of this path in every cultural context derives from its presence in the human world. The alternation of day and night, the loss and return of the sun and the moon, the seasonal cycle of plant life, all manifest the same drama of death and rebirth. Everything dies, but after an interval of rest everything is reborn and constitutes itself anew. The path from light into darkness and back again is symbolically equivalent to a sexual act followed by a birth, and sets a metaphoric seal of its own on all the things of this world. Death, whereby phenomenal realities vanish into darkness, signifies the journey into Hell, and thus equates with the act of penetration into the maternal uterus. There, in a dark and secluded space, the old life is burned away and new life begins to unfold. When this emerges into the light of day, death is vanquished. A new life is born, which at its conclusion sets out on its own journey into Hell, to maintain the cyclic renewal of the eternal drama of death and birth.

Two characteristics mark the path of light: on one hand, sexuality, in the form of procreation, birth, flowering, ripeness, decline, death, with all its concomitant imagery; on the other, the fact that this path is the lifestory of life itself. The path supplies life, in all its most varied manifestations,

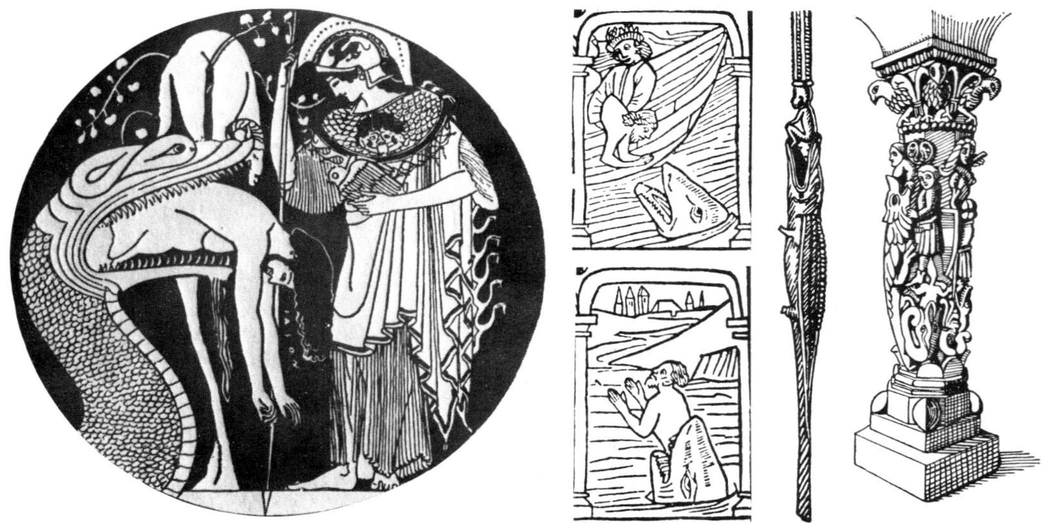

A sea-monster, devouring and spitting out man represents in many cultures the path from light to darkness and vice versa. From left to right: The return of Jason, attic bowl, 5th century B.C.; Jonas and the whale, Biblia pauperum, Augsburg 1471; In a sitting position (= rebirth) a candidate for initiation comes out of the jaws of a crocodile, ceremonial instrument from Rubiana; A column in the crypt of the dome of Freising showing a fish spitting out a man, 12th century.

with its most comprehensive biography. It is a biography that defines the course taken by every individual life, but also by every other phenomenon. Contrasts of light and shade lend their symbolism to all the multicoloured abstractions of the path; visually, they encapsulate its cyclic character by reducing it to two elements.

Human beings in every age, seeing all this in the world around them, have applied this same biographical pattern, this path of death and rebirth, to every aspect of cultural activity. Its successive stages have been used to describe their lives, their societies, their past, present and future. Whether this takes place on a microcosmic level only, or on the macrocosmic scale of the birth and death of whole worlds, is largely immaterial. What counts is the presence of the path as a socio-cultural pattern. In many cultures it serves the purpose of an initiation: a symbolic act that provides the individual, at a moment of transition from one segment of life to another, with a vivid image of change. The person to be initiated enters a form of symbolic darkness or underworld, there to cast off his previous identity. This is followed by his reception into a new or changed group within the human community.

In Christendom this function is performed by baptism. It brings the person baptized into contact with watery depths – a symbolic descent into infernal regions (p. 17) – before he is received, at the instant of "emergence", into the community of the faithful. This "emergence" from the dark waters signifies his rebirth as a Christian. The word "baptism" has a rarely used synonym – "photismos" – that recalls this connection. It means "illumination".[3]

In other cultures, including some in the South Pacific, this process is used to set the seal on the transition from youth to maturity. The young take part in a ritual that sends them symbolically through Hell. Candidates for initiation walk into the jaws of an effigy monster, stay within for a prescribed period, and emerge into the light as new-born adults (p. 19). They thereby cast off their childhood – symbolically kill it – in order to be reborn. The step into the dark is followed by the step into the light. Each candidate thus gains social recognition as a member of adult society.

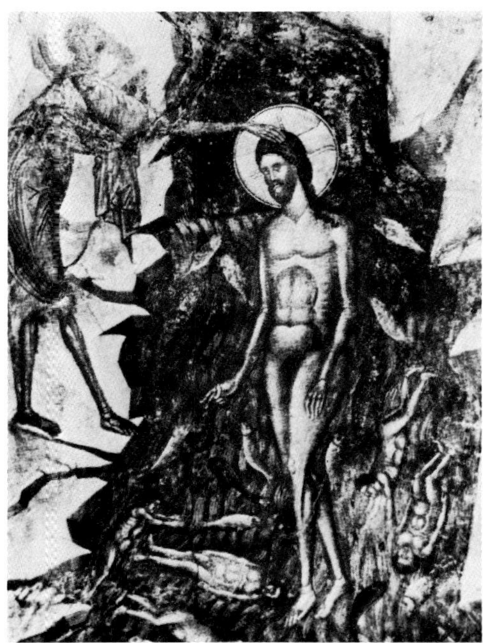

The baptism of Christ shown as descent into hell, cloister of Peribleptos, Greece.

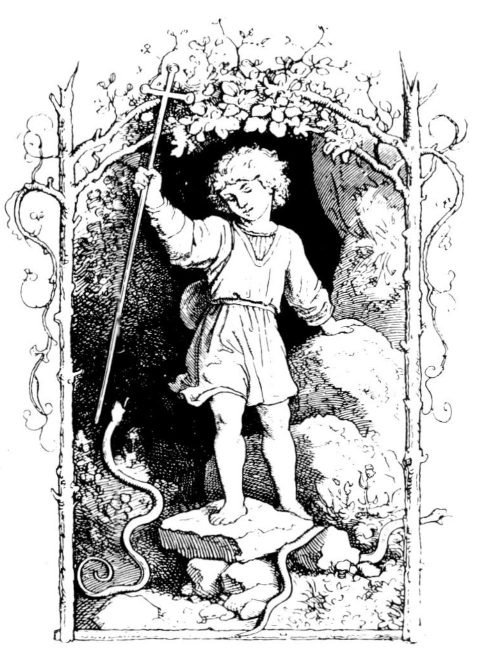

Ludwig Richter: It takes a lot to be a Christian. Killing the snake is the first step in the exit from darkness into light.

This brief digression into the general meaning of the motif of light and dark – the motif that reduces a dynamic process of vital development, initiation and physical self-constitution to its two essential marks – brings us back to the picture CLASS WAR. With its interplay of light and dark, its procession from one element to another, this work thus deals with an intercultural – because a universal human – theme. Here again, the central idea is the constitution of the human self, which takes place through liberation from darkness and movement towards the light. And, as if the artists were trying to emphasize the intercultural dimension, the young men in the procession in CLASS WAR clearly vary in origin. The international cast of figures underlines the universality of the theme, both in relation to the title and to the passage through darkness into light. The class war in CLASS WAR gives appropriate expression to a shared struggle as a reflection of the human impulse to constitute the self.

The dark-light motif – humanity in transition from one element to the other – stands at the core of the class war as presented here; and the remaining motifs define it further. They give content to the colour contrasts by complementing them – and the figures themselves – with living material. The two plant motifs, above all, define the process depicted as one of gradual growth. They announce it as the path of self-constitution: the attainment of a physically autonomous, self-directed life. This is, literally, underlined by the path of class war itself, defined by its red berries in green foliage as the path of ripeness and fruitfulness. Through this quality, the plant motifs allude to the goal pursued by these class warriors: maturation, self-constitution.

The association between ripeness and physical organization is also the theme of the circular leaf in the centre of CLASS WAR. In its quality as a perfect form – itself the product of constant growth – the leaf embodies the inherent dynamic of class war as a vital process of unfolding. Like the temporal process of leaf formation, which begins in the darkness of the bud and achieves perfection in light, class war too is a process of unfolding and emergence from the dark. In this sense, the class warriors themselves are "leaves": that is to say, a growing physical structure that attains autonomy in and with its own time. Finally, the drops of water on the leaf confer an explicitly osmotic character on the process whereby that structure unfolds and is established. They feed the organism, allow it to thrive, and keep it alive by preserving it from desiccation.

Whereas the plant metaphors in CLASS WAR allude to the physical characterization of the dark-light motif, the two pairs of eyes announce a further property of class war, one that concerns the mental orientation of every individual class warrior. The eyes, which look straight ahead without

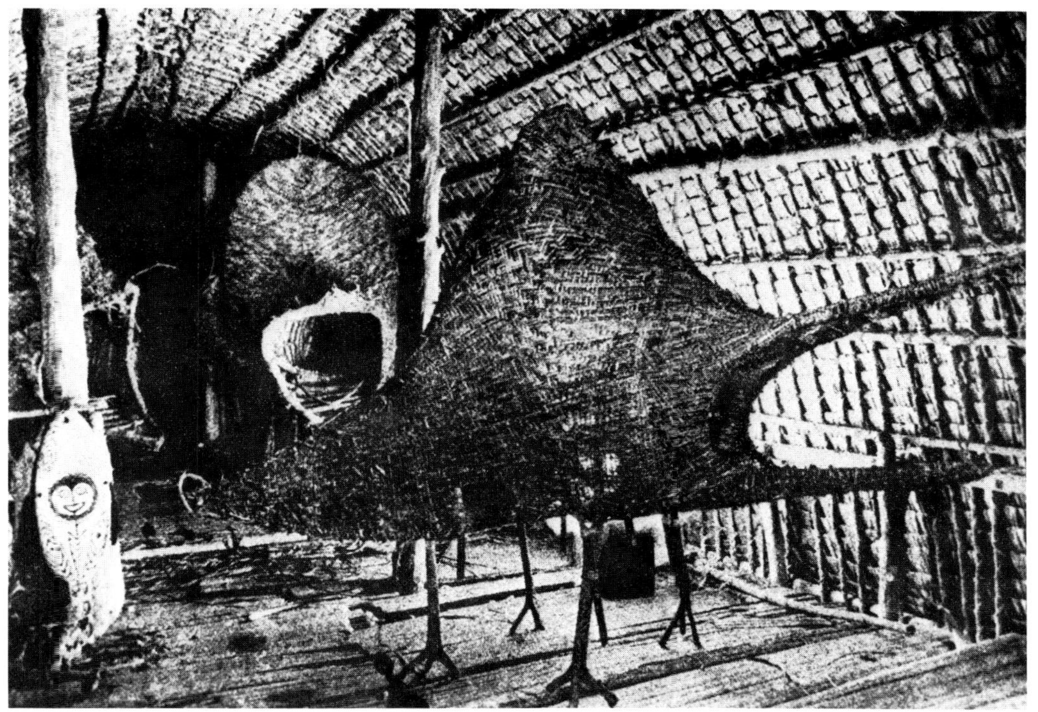

Kaiemunu-figures from New-Guinea in service for initiation.

making eye contact with the viewer, signal the direction of the gaze of all those involved. This is not a war effort directed against some enemey – an adversary, someone to look straight in the eye or to keep an eye on – but a fight to attain a goal: to progress along a still-untrodden path. Intent, unerring, undistracted, the two pairs of eyes stare straight ahead, as if no obstacle could ever stand in their way. They serve to define the class war as an unflagging endeavour to reach a place that still remains to be conquered: an endeavour that involves an element of conscious disregard; for the least sideways glance might disrupt progress and cripple the class war effort.

This eye motif is another of those that reappear in other cultures. An example from Nepal is shown on p. 49.

THE STAFF

Taken as a whole, what is happening in the foreground turns out to be an elaboration – and in particular a colouring – of the background motif. The procession of human beings towards the light, which in the background is merely quadrupled, is presented in the foreground as a unique event and elaborated through the use of a variety of colours and attributes. The staves, too, which the young men hold in their hands, are part of the elaboration of the motif. The plant metaphors reinforce the idea of physical self-constitution; the eyes set the single direction in which all must look; and the staves, too, play their part in completing the image of class war. After the physical organism and the sensory experience (the eyes), they supply the missing element of action. They introduce the ideas of erecting, supporting, acting, walking, fighting. Their significance, and their symbolic application, may be clarified by thinking of the traditional uses of a staff or a stick: the shepherd's crook, the bishop's crozier, the wayfarer's staff, the sceptre, the marshal's baton. One might add other customary usages of the word, in general staff, support staff, crisis staff: whether political or military, a staff exercises a function of leadership and direction.

The staff, like the light-dark motif, is an intercultural, universally human symbol. In many guises and forms, both as a sceptre and as a weapon, it appears on every continent (p. 21/22). It tends to make its appearances mostly in those places where human beings locate their identity and their home – a consequence of its physical nature, and in particular of its affinity to a tree trunk. In this it symbolizes the physical organism, in its aspect as a stem, a pillar, a structure, a support for the person who holds it. A staff, used instrumentally, thus has a number of meanings: it can serve as a prop to lean on, or as a symbol of sovereignty; it can be used for defence; or – as a stem – it can represent the central mainstay of individual life (and here it comes close to the symbolism of the Tree of Life). And this is the area of value and meaning to which the staves in the triptych CLASS WAR, MILITANT, GATEWAY belong. In CLASS WAR, they emphasize support and forward movement; in MILITANT, they assume the function of sceptres.

As the staves that all the figures hold are ordinary roofing battens, they are free from any elitist overtones. The staff is not used here to subjugate anyone else; nor does it represent any kind of exclusive resource, inaccessible to others. In symbolic terms, this is a democratic implement, both in its ease of acquisition and in the form of rule to which it lays claim. This form of anti-hierarchy is illustrated by another of the artists' pictures, with

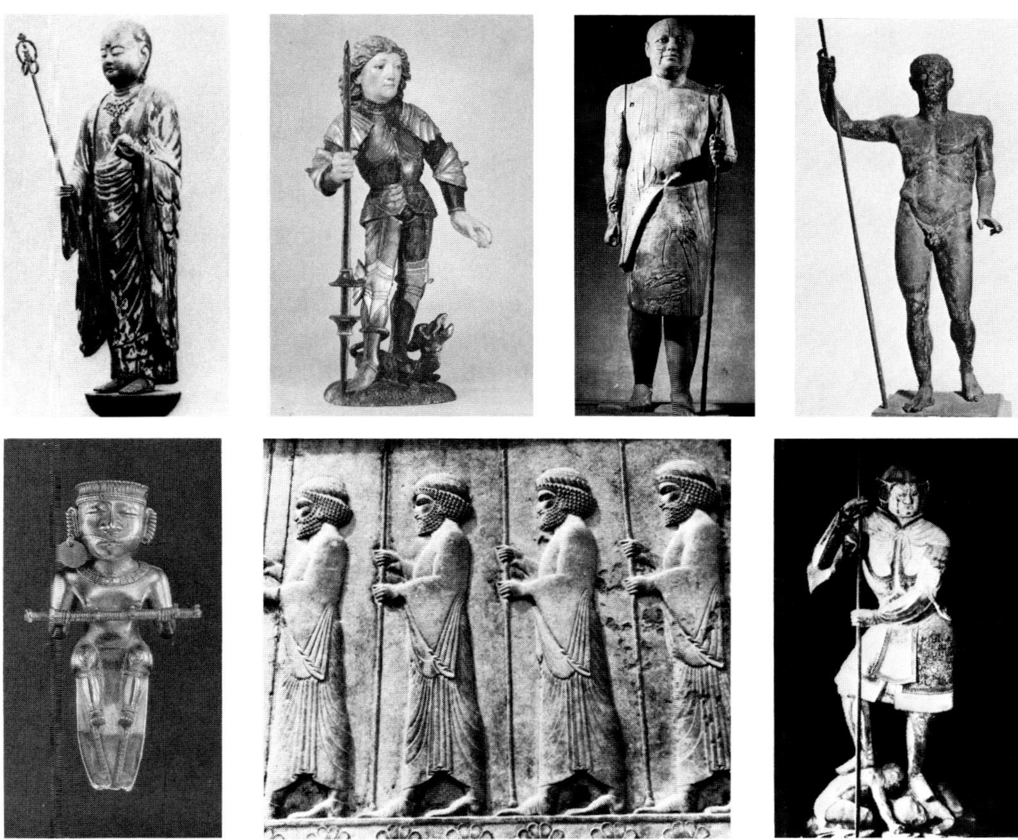

The staff as an intercultural symbol of rule, dignity and individual autarky. From left to right, from the top to the bottom (classified into countries, for more information see notes): Japan, Southern German or Austrian, Egypt, Rome, Columbia, Persia, Japan;
next page: India, New Zealand, Mexico, Germany, Indonesia, Pacific, Marquesa-Islands, Kamerun, North America, France, Spain, Thailand, Greece.
(see also next page)

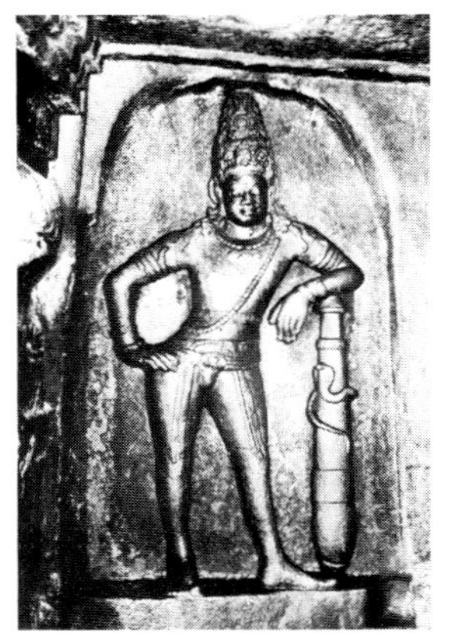 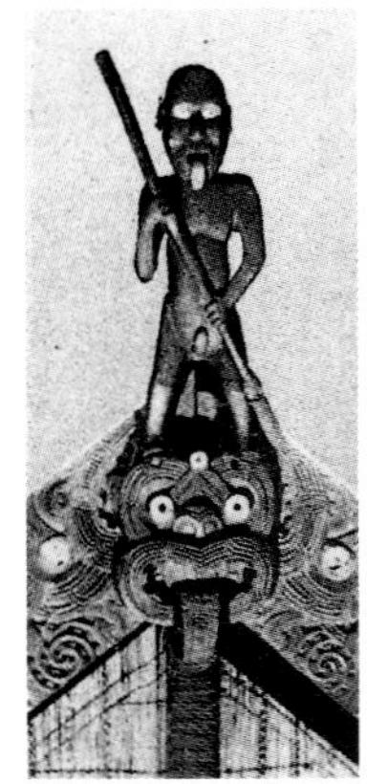 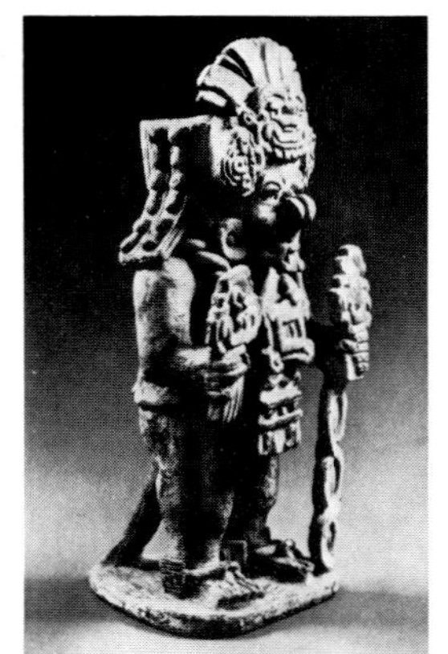 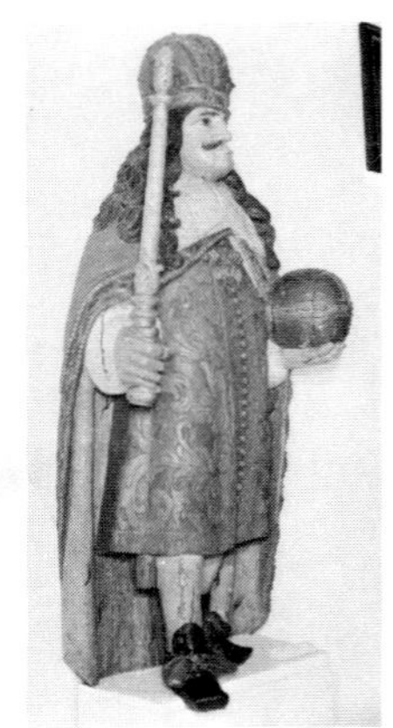

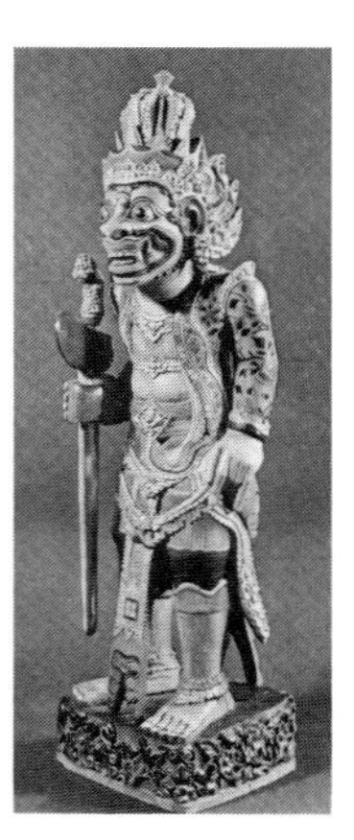 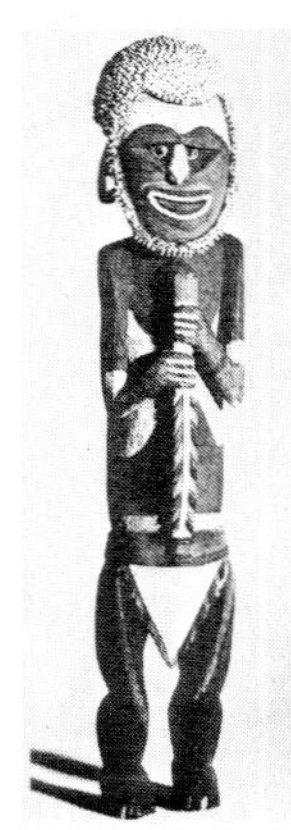 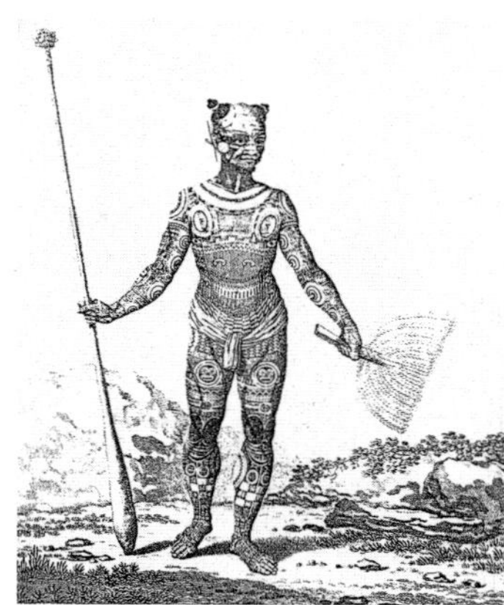 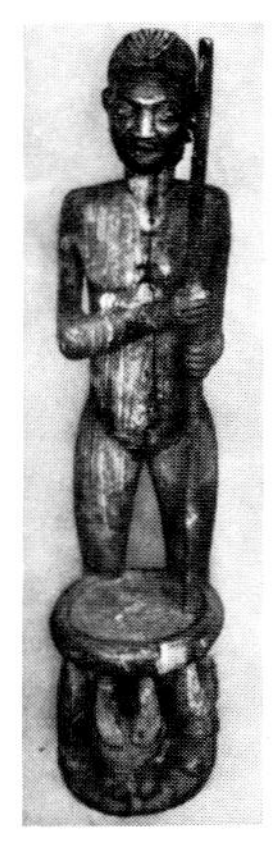 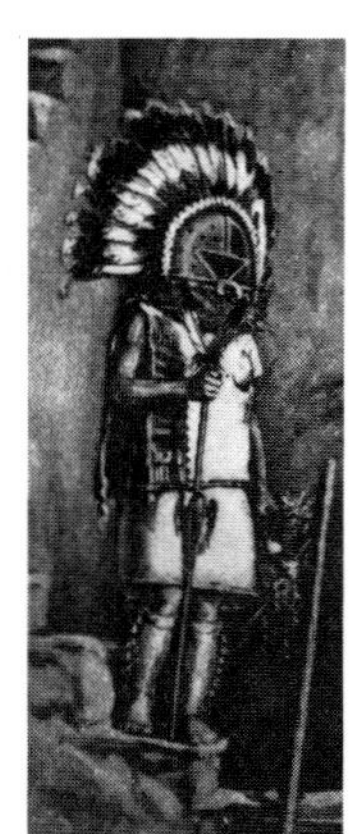

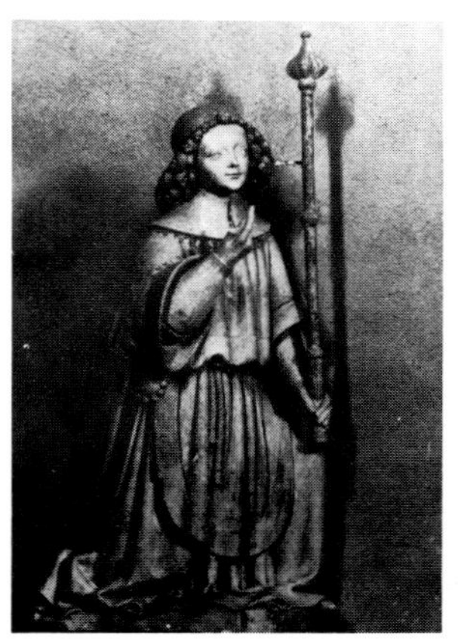 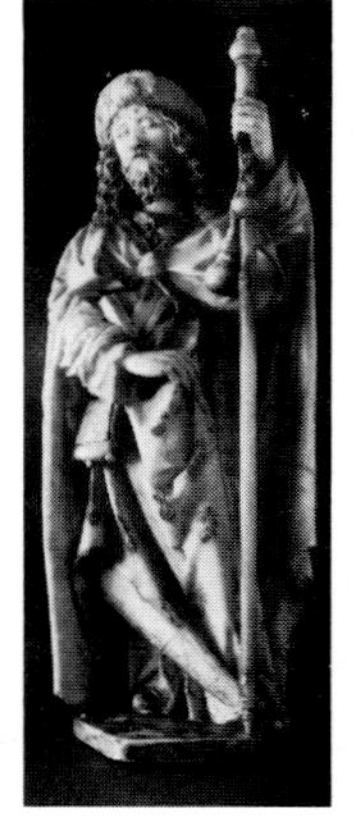 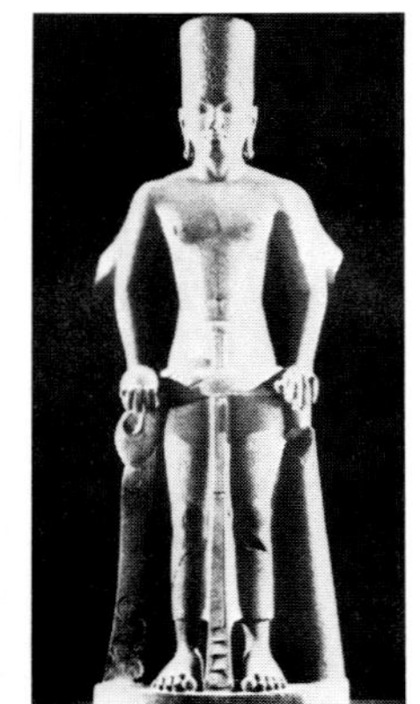 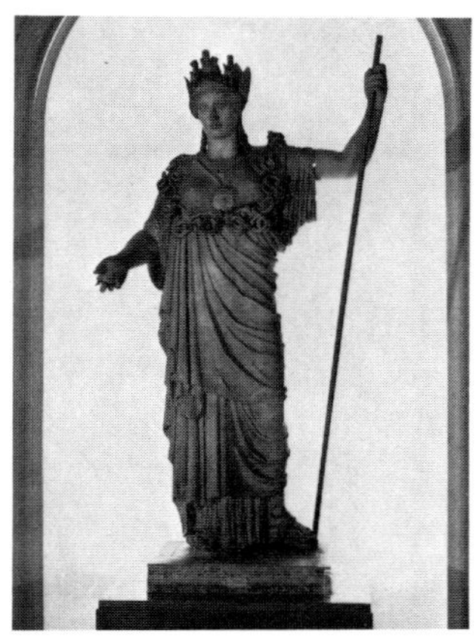

Notes see preceding page.

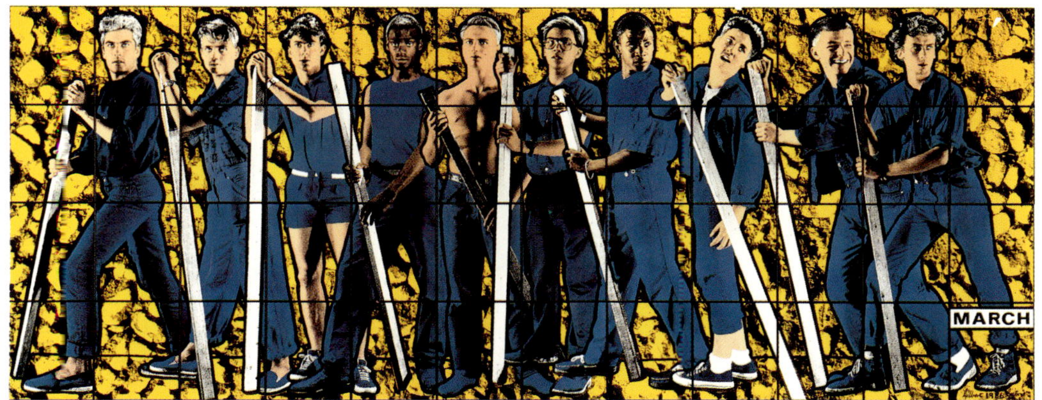

MARCH, 1986, 242×606 cm.

the title MARCH (p. 23). Here, too, young men hold roofing battens in
their hands as staves. The stony background, like the battens, alludes to the
deliberately democratic nature of the picture. That is to say, the everyday
nature of the metaphors points to the exclusion of exclusivity, whether in
content or in form. The form of rule that is called for here is human
autarky: the unfolding of individual and autonomous life. In this function,
the staff is a generalized symbol of its own use to the individual. The point
here is its symbolic value, as a growth stem, as a support, and as a weapon.
It represents all the different working resources that individuals can place in
the service of the constitution of the self. The staff signifies that every
person, in order to live independently, needs a working utensil, a means of
production that he himself controls, and whose use is a matter for him to
decide. By this means he defines himself as a sovereign, self-determining
individual.

Through its various motifs, CLASS WAR opens up the general theme.
Dark and light are used to indicate the direction of the path, which is
adorned with fruits in anticipation of the goal towards which the class
warriors are moving: physical perfection, ripeness. The staring eyes stress
the unanimity with which all concerned look the same way; the staves
allude to their individual weapons, in the sense both of an implement and a
sceptre. The background repeats the central event of CLASS WAR, the
endeavor to pass from darkness into light, and does so through an image
that is derived from everyday reality. It thus clarifies the identity of the
class that is concerned here: that of people in general. The class, in CLASS
WAR, is everyone.

The struggle itself as an event – its dynamic factor – finds expression in CLASS WAR. Both the warriors and their war are presented in some detail. What remains to be clarified is the image, the aim, the objective, for which they fight. Although the fruit-laden path suggests that the essence of this is physical ripeness, and the pattern of lighting suggests a progression towards the light, the aim still awaits its own appropriate formulation. One might thus logically expect the wings of the triptych to incorporate a continuation of CLASS WAR, either in GATEWAY or in MILITANT. The obvious place to look for this would be on the right, as CLASS WAR itself reads from left to right. But the order of the wings cannot be determined from the public showings of the triptych that have taken place. CLASS WAR has consistently held the central position; but the relative positions of the other two pictures have never been finally settled. They have both been shown to left and to right of the central image.[4]

This interchangeability of the two wings is certainly intentional rather than a sign of casualness. It is characteristic of the art of Gilbert & George that the artists define it as sculpture, in the sense that it is an autonomous image, a self-sufficient figure.[5] They see each of their pictures as a self-contained work without reference to any other. Although several pictures may correspond to a single complex of meaning, each individual work is not a fragment of a whole, incomplete without the others. Each picture is designed to work as a statement either alone or in conjunction. CLASS WAR illustrates this: as a picture that denotes the activity of a struggle, a war, it is self-sufficient; in conjunction with GATEWAY and MILITANT, it states the theme of a triptych. The same goes for the other two pictures.

The possibility that either GATEWAY or MILITANT can follow directly upon CLASS WAR is also kept open by the nature of the respective compositions. This is indicated by, for example, the figures at the front of the procession in CLASS WAR. Close inspection reveals that the first four figures are not stepping out, as the rest are, but standing still. As the very same number of standing figures is presented in MILITANT (p. 30/31) – this time large and dominant within the picture – it would be natural to place that picture immediately after CLASS WAR. There are, however, logical grounds for supposing that this position should be assigned to GATEWAY (p. 26/27). Above all, the white upper garments worn, as in the right-hand half of CLASS WAR, by almost all the figures in GATEWAY suggest a continuation of the class war. Another feature that the two works have in common is the large number of figures that they contain. Again –

and importantly – there is the position of the title, which in GATEWAY, unlike the other two pictures, appears at the top. This supplies an indirect analogy to CLASS WAR, where, four times over, a path leads up to a light-filled gateway: in GATEWAY, the title itself occupies a corresponding position. These features suggest that the class struggle that begins in CLASS WAR is continued in GATEWAY.

First, however, the picture itself. As with CLASS WAR, its whole length is occupied by a line of young men. Here, however, they are not walking, and the majority lack their staves. Their postures vary: mostly with hands on knees or thighs, with torsos bent forward, and looking slightly upward, they seem to be raising themselves into an erect position. Their postures, with the upward gaze hinting at further development, embody the principle of rising and erecting. And as if to underline this process by presenting the form with which it will end, the outsize and fully upright figures of the artists flank the scene. Rising through the whole height of the picture, standing squarely with staves in their hands, they enrich the picture's title with the notion of the entrance to a citadel. They attend, like sentinels at a gate, as the action proceeds between them.

Just as in CLASS WAR, the figure theme is accompanied and paraphrased by a plant theme. Behind the young men, between them and the background, is a line of bushes, laden with blossom, which provide a variation on the given theme of unfolding and upward surging. They signal an opening towards the light, but also a gradual, twining growth. The figures do the same. They unfold in the light as their postures and their white garments suggest. Figure and plant motifs thus interact within the ongoing process of self-constitution.

The background, finally, affords a view of the terrain beyond the gateway itself: this is the city. An urban panorama in bright daylight fills the entire width of the picture. This too is a continuation of CLASS WAR. That showed an underground structure, the underside of the city, with its passageway leading upwards; GATEWAY shows the city as it appears in the light. The city is first perceived at the threshold between Above and Below.

The gateway in GATEWAY takes up the theme of CLASS WAR twice over, and carries the struggle into its next phase. Through the postures of the figures, their gradual rise and blossoming, it reflects the next stage after the entry into the light, the emergence from darkness that CLASS WAR prepared but did not accomplish. But – and this seems initially to conflict with the usual metaphorical use of light – on this threshold between darkness and daylight the light comes upon the figures less as a culmination of the path already traversed than as a shock, at the moment when their self-

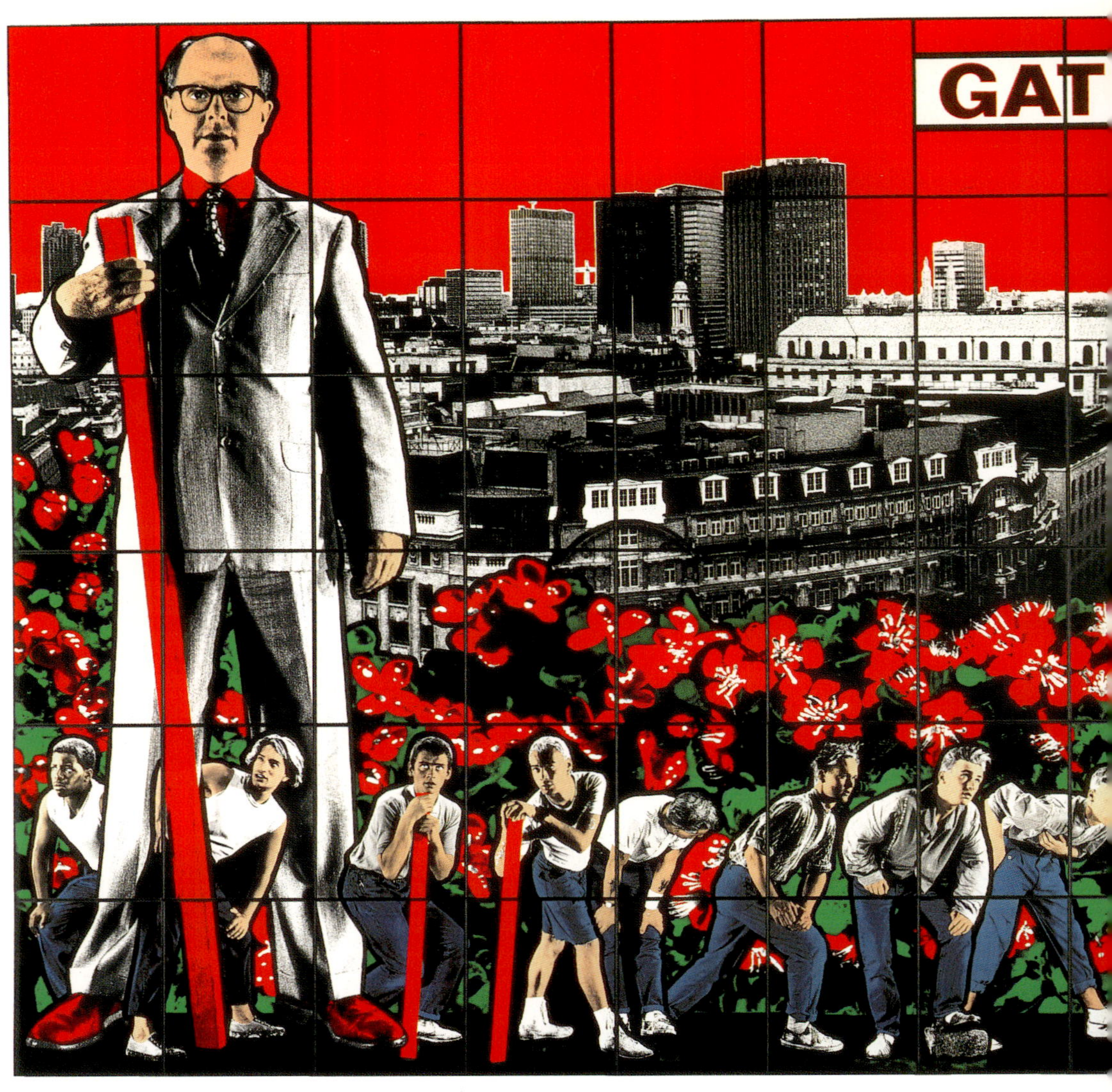

GATEWAY from CLASS WAR, MILITANT, GATEWAY, 1986, 363 x 758 cm.

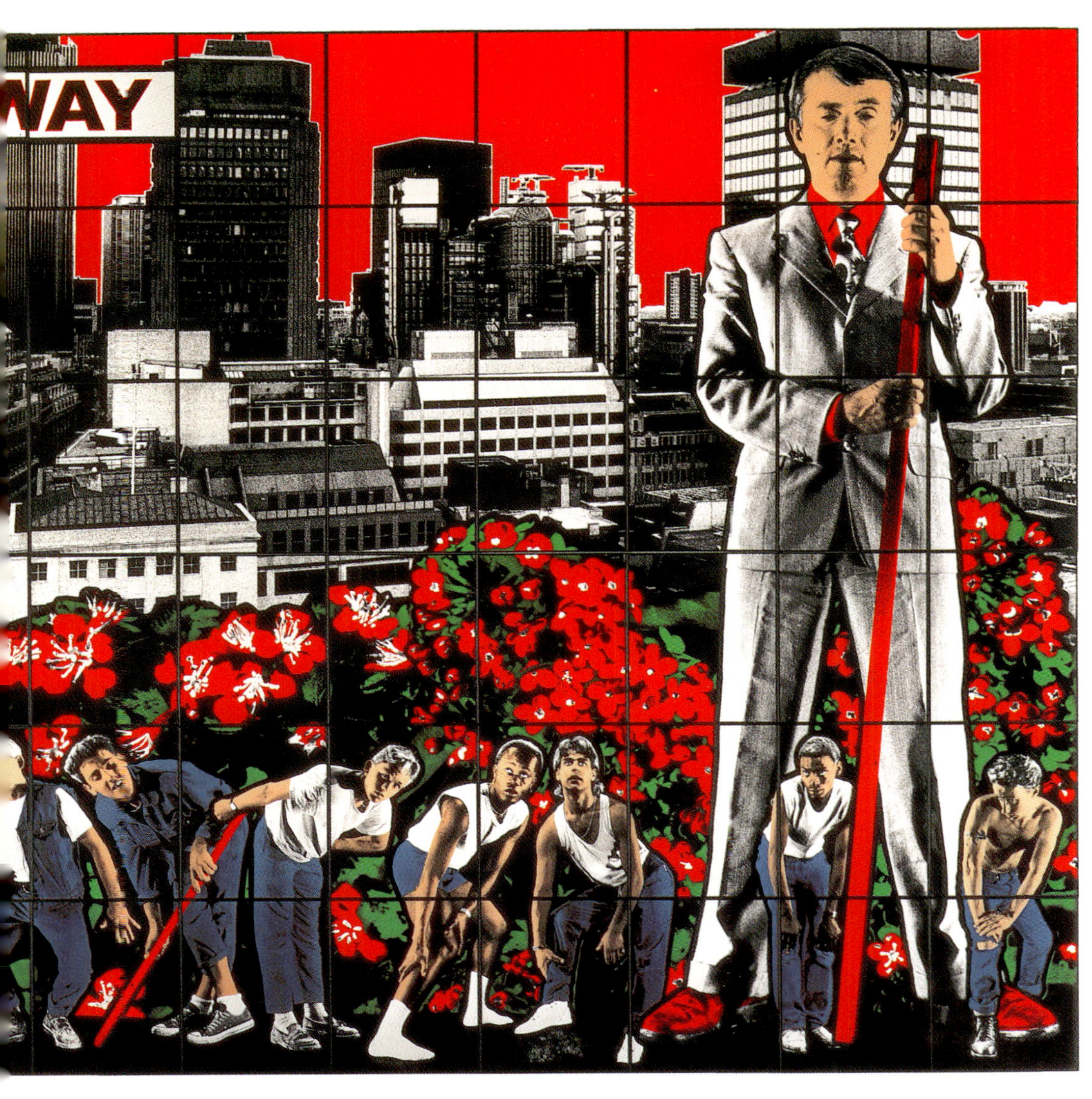

WAY

constitution at last becomes conscious. Mere bright light is not at all the goal of the struggle. It is – to speak figuratively – only a lure; it is the sense-based underpinning of the struggle that began in CLASS WAR. In this sense, the gateway marks the threshold between mere impulse and the awareness of the self-constitution that each must achieve for himself. The background of GATEWAY opens up the wider space of class war, the locus of the evolutionary growth that is shown in the foreground. The city is the space in which, in future, all those concerned will operate and act.

MILITANT

Just as connections may be traced between CLASS WAR and MILITANT, but also between CLASS WAR and GATEWAY, the same can be done between the two wing panels themselves. Notably, the figures of the artists in GATEWAY are directly analogous to the four young men in MILI-TANT (p. 30/31): in size – both sets of figures occupy the entire height of the picture – and also in presentation. Both groups stand upright, facing the viewer, and hold staves; these are not wayfarers' staves, like those in CLASS WAR, but static supports. Their direction is parallel to the axis of the body.

The differences between MILITANT and the other two pictures are also evident. The artists, who are the flanking figures in GATEWAY and the two pairs of eyes in CLASS WAR, are absent here; and so are the multiple "small" young men. Instead, the viewer is confronted by a unified group of four (literally) grown men. The background, however, retains the plant and urban motifs common to the other pictures: behind the feet of the young men are two horizontally placed branches with red thorns, and the background is filled by another urban landscape. In the dominant, central part this has been tilted through 90 degrees; at either side it lies horizontal.

One notable feature of MILITANT is the presentation of the four young men. This is the only panel of the triptych in which all the figures lack the white upper garment, and the only one in which they all rise to the full height of the picture. Surprisingly, the plant motif here does not run across the whole width but is broken in the centre. It thus divides the figure group into two smaller units, each unified by the branch behind it.

If we regard MILITANT as the "last" picture in the triptych, it is tempting to suppose that it reverts to the starting point of CLASS WAR. Here, as there, the young men are naked to the waist; the white garment

makes its appearance in between. The difference lies in the scale and –
particularly – in the posture of the figures. Those in CLASS WAR walk;
those in MILITANT stand. The specific identity of MILITANT can thus
be established in terms of similarities and dissimilarities to the other pictures. Evidently, a number of young men have matured into a unified
group, which has taken a stand and thus, like the artists in GATEWAY,
attained bodily wholeness. This whole is MILITANT, as announced by the
title, because here a physical self-constitution has matured into an alert and
upright posture of self-defence. MILITANT stands for the human capacity
and potential for self-assertion. It has transformed the upright gait of the
young men in CLASS WAR – temporarily disrupted in GATEWAY by the
"shock" of the light – into an equally upright stance, freed from the white
garment. After successive stages of building up, man experiences his upright
destiny. The title, MILITANT, is a declaration of readiness to assert and to
defend this self-earned self-constitution.

The militant steadfastness of the figures in MILITANT is emphasized
by the plant motif. Two horizontally placed branches with red thorns are
visual expressions of the title. The reference to a "stem", or a branch, with
defensive thorns, elucidates the relation between the established physical
organism and its outwardly visible protection. And as if to transpose these
characteristics into the space in which human life thrives, the city follows
both the horizontal and the vertical orientations of the plant motif. As a
human habitat, it is characterized by the direction of defence and the direction of growth that are common to all physical organisms. In this it recalls
the fortifications of medieval cities, with their horizontal walls and vertical
watchtowers. In terms of the triptych, this means that in CLASS WAR
man begins to aspire to self-constitution, the attainment of full selfhood,
and that he attempts this in GATEWAY before attaining it in MILITANT.
Militancy signifies self-assertion and self-constitution. And so the wayfarer's staff, which in CLASS WAR was still a support, has transformed itself
in MILITANT into a sceptre. Here man is the sovereign of his own existence. There is, however, a condition attached to this: he must lay aside the
white garment, the outward show. What this means will emerge from the
section that follows.

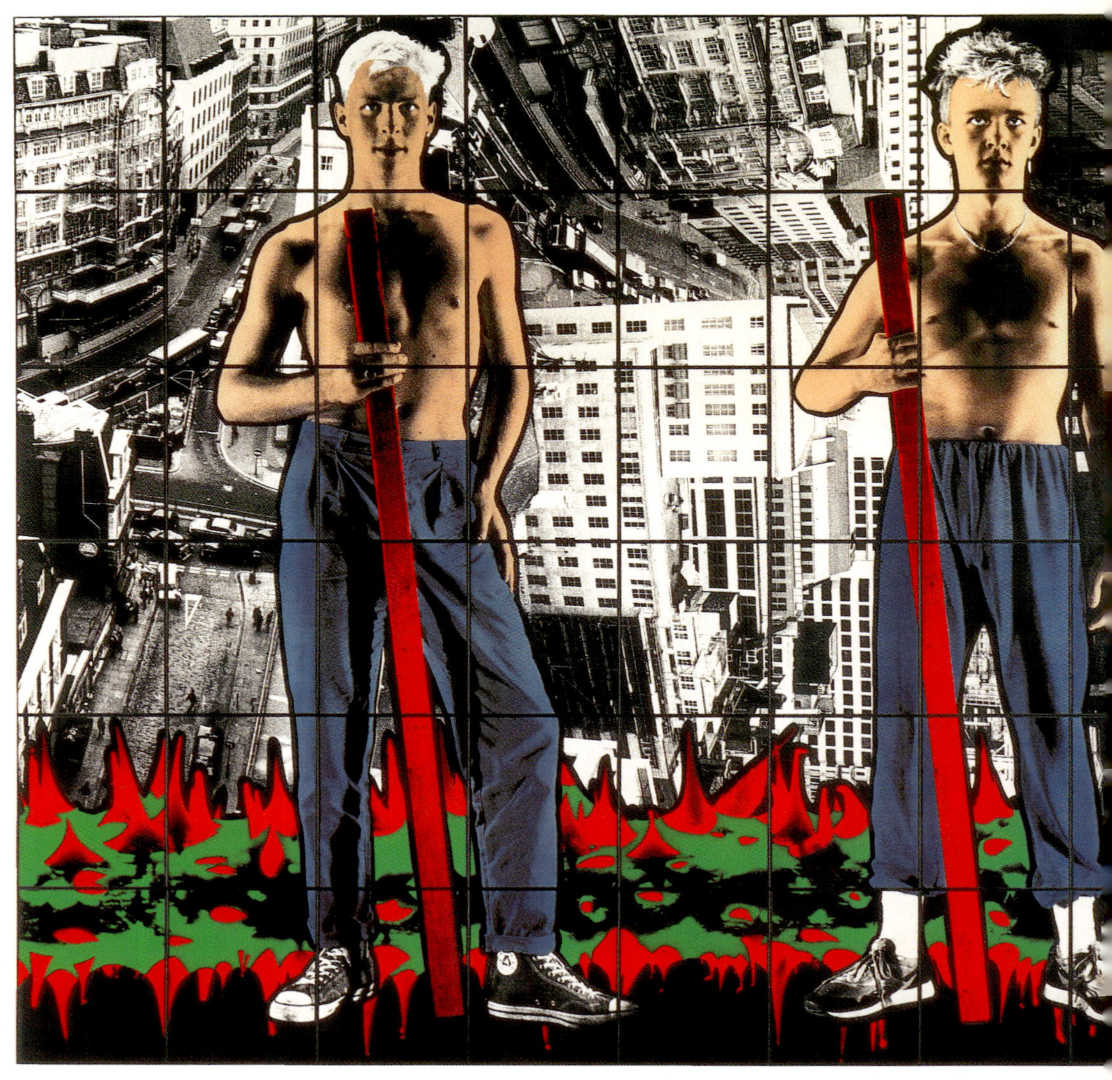

MILITANT from CLASS WAR, MILITANT, GATEWAY, 1986, 363 x 758 cm.

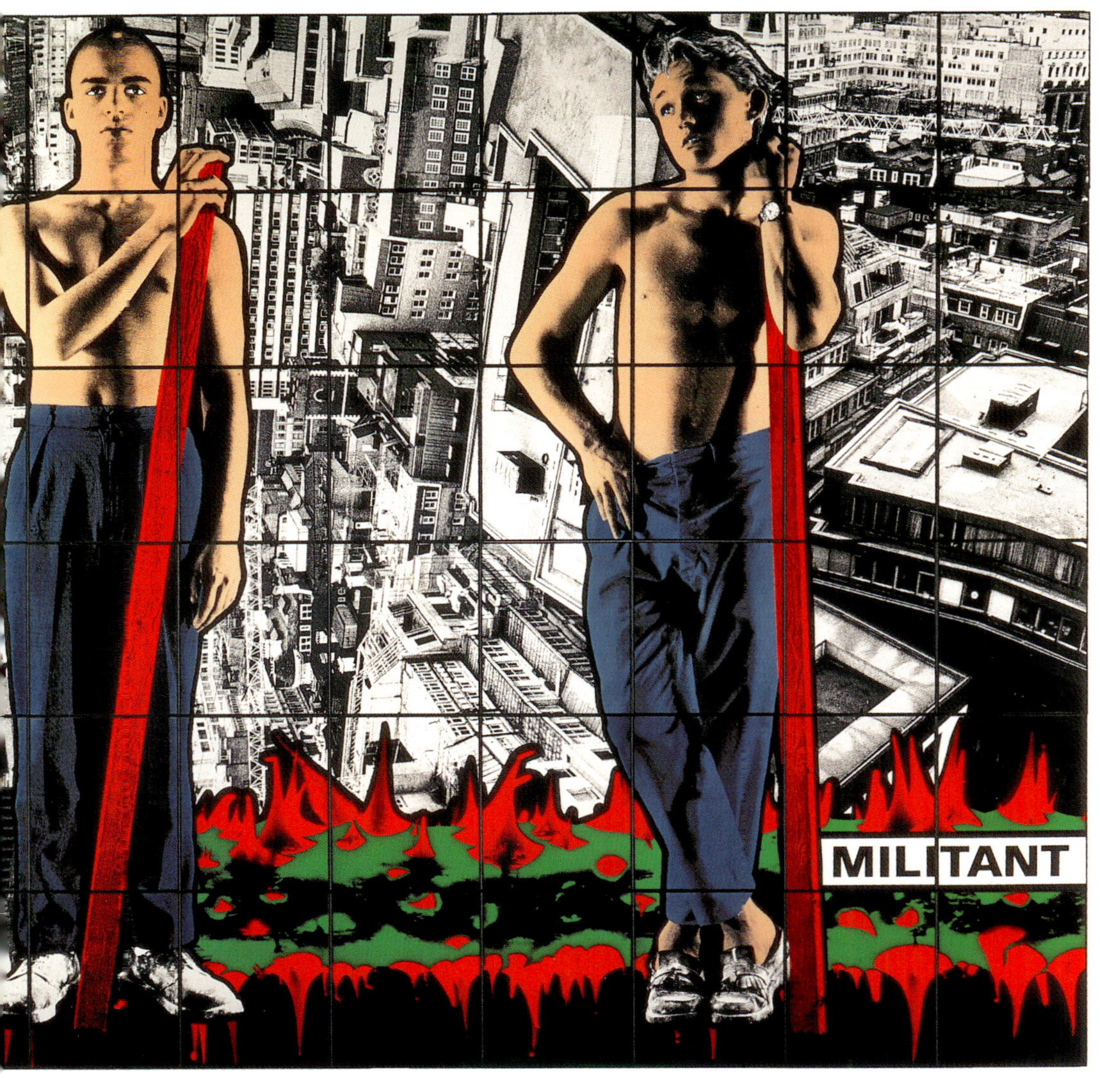

MILITANT

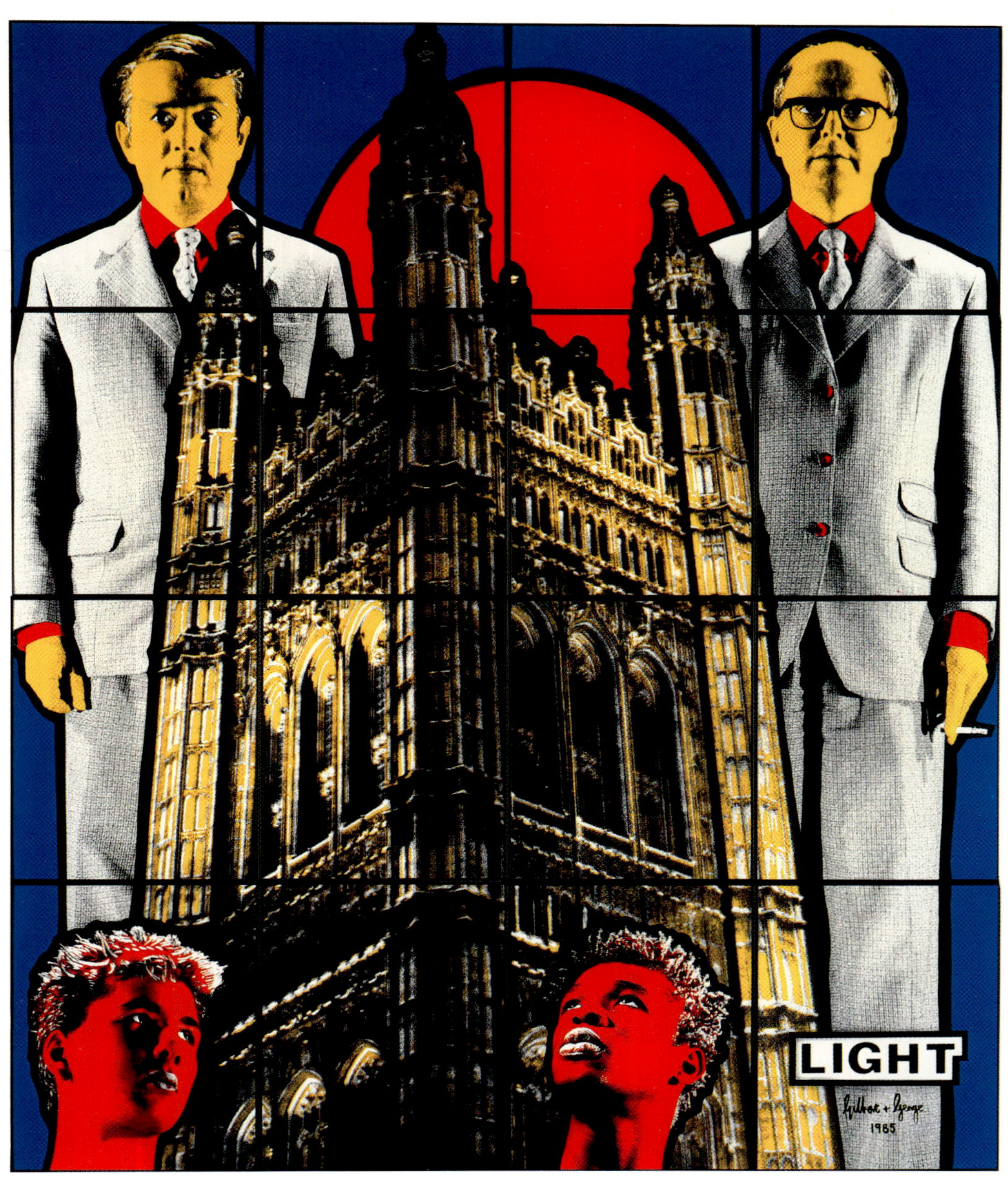

LIGHT, 1985, 241 x 201 cm.

THE LIGHT

That concludes the description of the three pictures in the triptych, its components, its motifs and its specific properties. In addition, the individual pictures are linked by sequences that reinforce and further define the expressive force of the triptych as a whole. Aside from the plant and city motifs, a prominent feature is the conspicuous play of light and dark on the figures, which enables the three pictures to be read as a sequence articulated by the specific distinctions it establishes. CLASS WAR displays both light and dark; GATEWAY, with a single exception, shows only the light; and MILITANT shows only dark, bare torsos. This looks at first as if the human procession were engaged in a constant rise and fall. At the beginning and at the end, it is in the dark; in between, it dwells in the light.

However, the bare torsos in MILITANT have little in common with those in CLASS WAR. Here there is no simple play of contrasts, as in CLASS WAR, where the light denoted Above and Below: dark for Below, light and light garments for Above. In MILITANT, by contrast, there are subtle distinctions: the place where the four men stand is not below the city, as the background in CLASS WAR suggests; and the lighting has undergone a radical change. CLASS WAR and GATEWAY lead us to suppose that the source of the light is a disembodied beam that simply scatters light on the figures; but MILITANT resists such a conception. The young men here do not stand in the dark; they are neither bathed in light – wearing white – nor shrouded in darkness. The point lies elsewhere. Here light is no longer disembodied but itself a body. Light in MILITANT is no longer an element superior to man – shining on him – but man himself. Man is light, a body of light: not in isolation from matter but through and with matter.

This treatment of light involves the issue of defining light. Is light, scientifically speaking, only a phenomenon that supplies brightness in a range of wavelengths? Or is light, symbolically speaking, every being that takes on form and can thus be known? In other words: does light assist us to lighten the darkness by extracting experience from concealment; or is every form and every being already visible experience, concrete awareness, and hence light? The picture LIGHT (p. 32), by Gilbert & George, shows the conception of light that the artists favour. Here, unmistakably, a minutely structured and differentiated architectural form presents itself to the viewer as light. Structure, especially when elaborately formed and finished, constitutes in a literal sense the Body of Light.

The same happens in the triptych to the human body: firstly in that mere brightness, in the form of a white garment, is characterized as no more than a stimulus; and secondly in that the constitution of the human self is inserted into the picture by presenting man as an upright, "dark" figure. The state of being drawn to and clad in undifferentiated brightness, which prevails in CLASS WAR and GATEWAY, is followed in MILITANT by a reversal. Here man is no longer stepping towards a light; he himself, with and through his own upright body, personifies light.

To emphasize the startling nature of this conception of light, and to understand the significance of light as a physical body, it must be seen in conjunction with the opposite view of light, which is also the traditional one. To pose the question in general terms, within the historical context of Western civilization: where, and in what pictures, is it possible to find a manifestation of the traditional conception of light, its relationship with human values, and its own symbolic value? One obvious answer lies in an image that, in countless variations over the centuries, has constantly drawn upon the interplay of light and dark: that of the Last Judgment. This theme has made a powerful contribution to the traditional understanding of light and of its counterpart, darkness, in Western civilization. The image of the Last Judgment, which centres on the final separation of human beings into the just and the unjust, the good and the evil, by Christ as the Judge of the World, and which shows them respectively entering Paradise and being committed to Hell, has always depended on the value distinction between brightness and darkness. Its division into Heaven and Hell, which are the realms of light and dark respectively, marks the definitive statement of the traditional idea of light as a metaphor for salvation and redemption (p. 35).

An illustration of the effectiveness of this image – and also an ideal contrast with the triptych by Gilbert & George – is a Last Judgment painted in the mid nineteenth century by John Martin. Not only in its relation to light but also in other ways, this is a highly illuminating document. Martin encompassed his theme so comprehensively that there are three paintings in all: another analogy with the triptych. The three now hang side by side in the Tate Gallery in London. The central painting, THE LAST JUDGMENT (p. 37), shows Christ seated in judgment. To his right and left, the good and the wicked are consigned to eternal life and to eternal damnation respectively. The paintings to either side represent the future lives of the saved and of the damned. On the right – as seen from the judgment seat – Paradise is shown in an extensive view of THE PLAINS OF HEAVEN (p. 36), with, in the far distance, a glimpse of the Heavenly City of Jerusalem. To the left, on THE GREAT DAY OF HIS WRATH (p. 36), the damned fall into the flames of Hell.

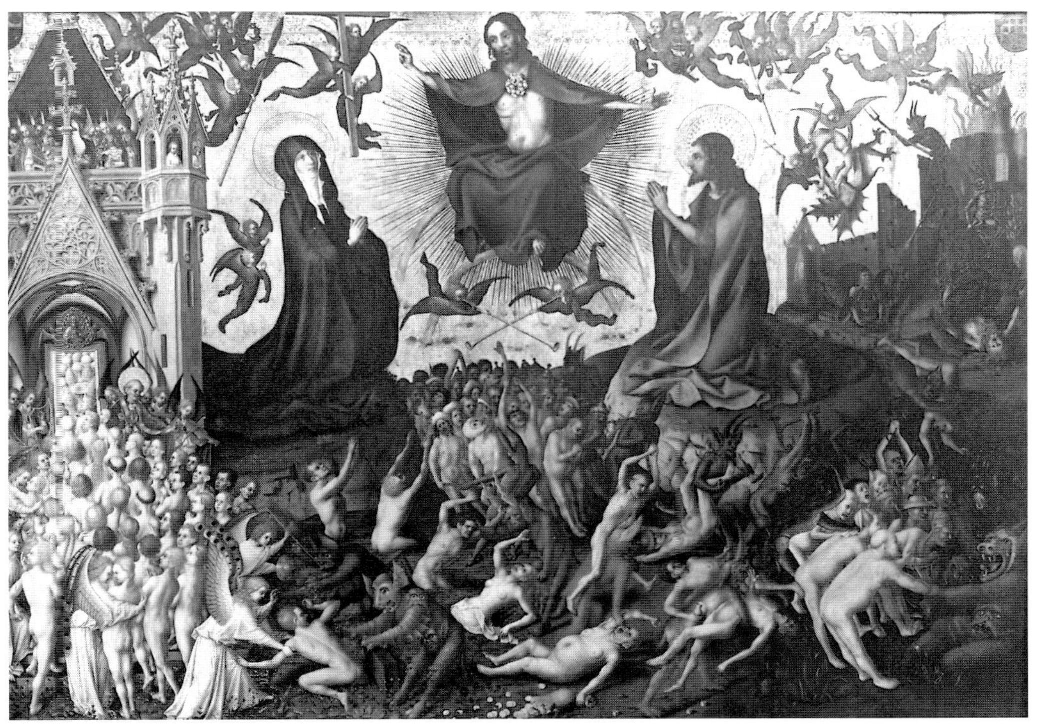

Stephan Lochner: The Last Judgement, about 1440, (Wallraf-Richartz-Museum, Cologne).

There are other reasons for associating Martin's work with that by Gilbert & George, so that a number of converging perspectives lead to the triptych. The first reason is thematic. Of course, class war and Last Judgment are markedly distinct as subjects; what unites them is the fact that both are about salvation. The Last Judgment turns on the salvation or otherwise of human beings when they have been resurrected, when the world has come to an end, and when eternal life has begun; the class war – and not only Gilbert & George's class war – also refers to the salvation of mankind, but before death and not after it. The historical class war, as formulated by Marx and Engels, has as its object the removal of class distinctions on earth: to set people free not in Heaven but here below. By its nature, the class war relies on an idea of salvation analogous to that of the Last Judgment: the deliverance of mankind from evil, oppression, and slavery. The difference is that the Last Judgment frees, and also segregates,

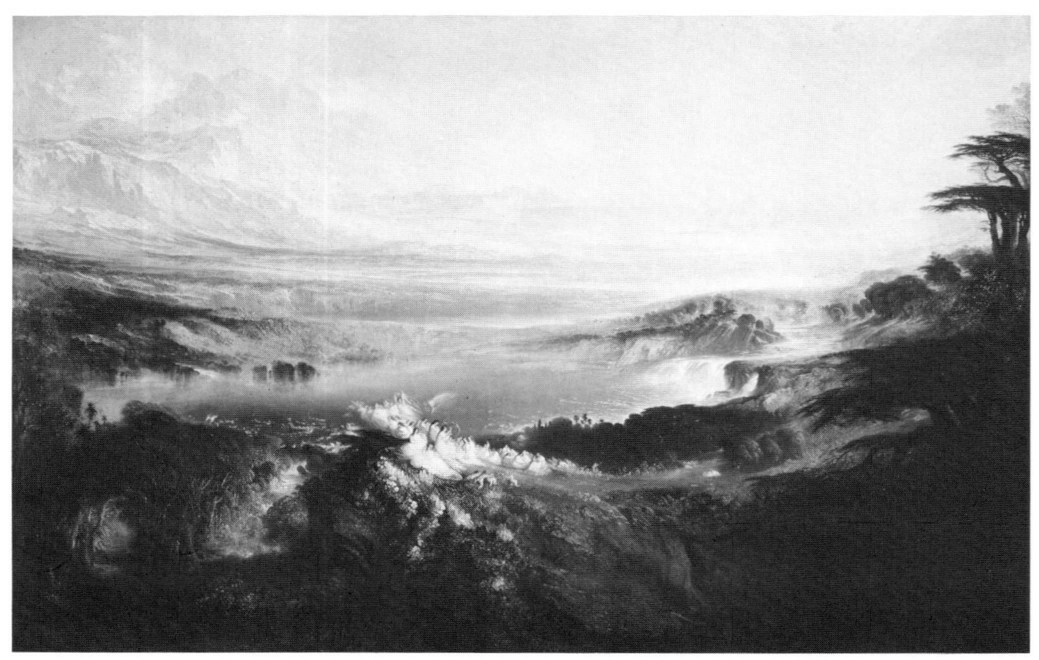

John Martin: The Plains of Heaven, Tate Gallery, London.

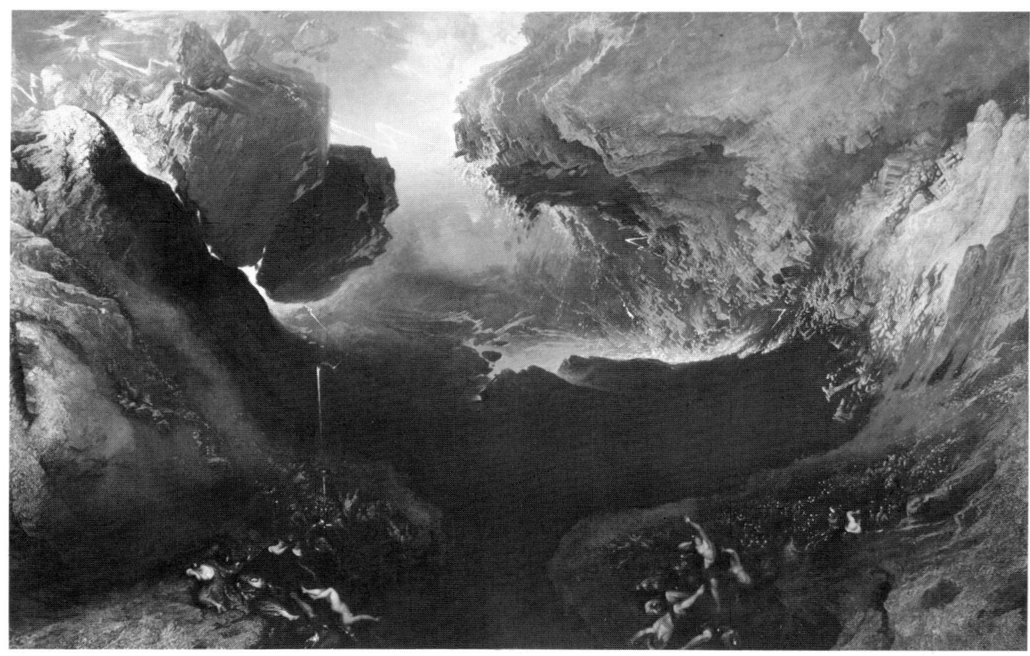

John Martin: The Great Day of His Wrath, Tate Gallery, London.

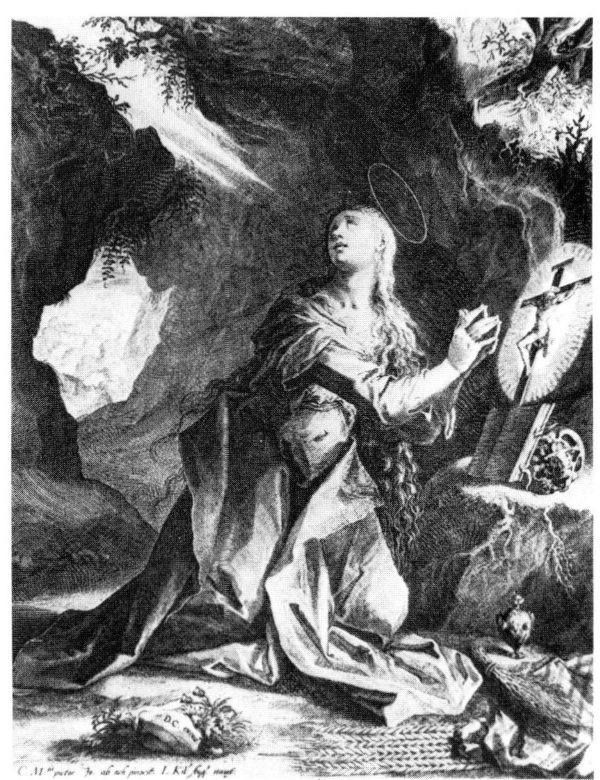

Light serving divine powers. Lucas Kilian after Hans von Aachen: Madgalene penitent in front of the cross, after 1591.

The halo of a saint, and the dazzling light of an extraterrestrial being in a science-fiction film, exemplify the magic of this metaphorical use of light (p. 39). It lives and feeds upon the mental existence of the "Unexplained", the "Other", the "Metaphysical" or the "Ineffable", outside and above the human and empirical world. The workers' song, "Brothers to the Sun, to Freedom!" uses it by directly associating human liberty with the radiance of the sun. The Nazis also made it work for them. On great occasions, Albert Speer used gigantic searchlights to project what were called "cathedrals of light" into the night sky (p. 40). The phrase "cathedrals of light" itself introduces the suggestion of some sacred and supraterrestrial power, and of an architecture that transcends the human realm. Even where the traditional metaphor of light was applied exclusively to earthly matters – as it was in the light of the Enlightenment – supernatural qualities still clung to it. Reason would illuminate all; reason would set things in an entirely objec-

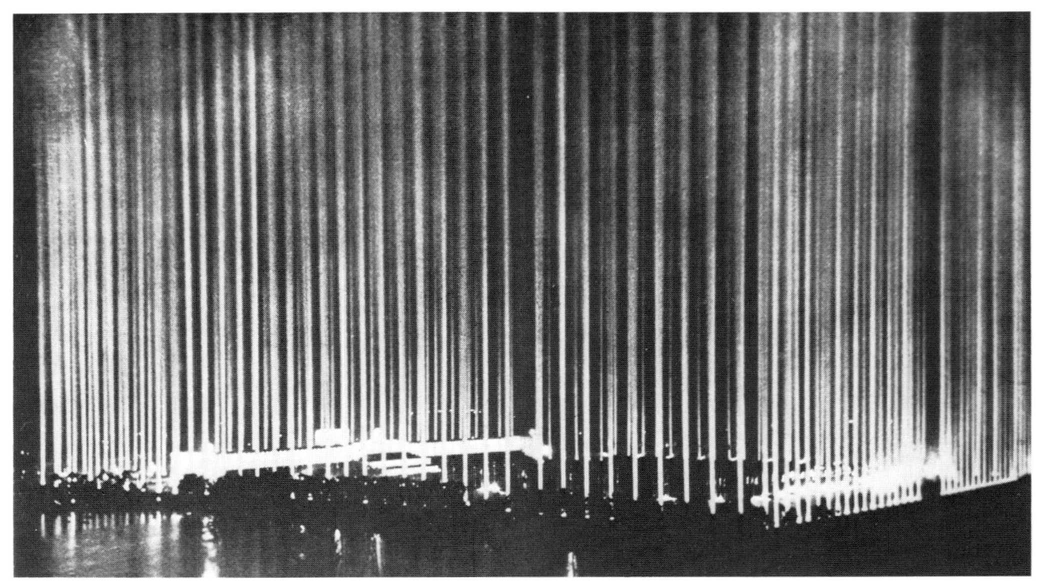

Dome of light by Albert Speer during the Reichsparteitag on 11th September 1937 in Nuremberg.

tive light; and mankind would be freed from the darkness of a traditional view of the universe. What this meant, however, was that reason itself assumed the supernatural aura of the divine and the transcendental. This sprang principally from its claim to omnipotence. Reason regarded knowledge as its own exclusive province, accepting no other form of knowledge on equal terms. Reason exalted itself by consigning others to Hell.

Gilbert & George's triptych favours an exactly opposite concept of light. Here, brightness is purely a stimulus, a lure; darkness represents human self-constitution. This represents a liberation from prevalent conceptions of light and at the same time the acceptance of another. Man in his progressively constituted and complete physical nature represents light; and the supraterrestrial and extraterrestrial light – the white garment – is nothing but an illusion. Only when he has laid it aside – and thus symbolically abandoned his own subjection to a being outside himself – can he become a ruler, a sovereign, a light in his own right. There is a solidly political aspect to the metaphorical use of light in this triptych. It symbolizes freedom from the mistaken fear that man's self-constitution is prevented by some uncomprehended, inexplicable power. It does not matter what he blames for this, whether a political system, or economic circumstances, or a failed socialization process: to believe in any ruling, regulative, oppressive power is to be blinded by an external light. That light may exert a magical attraction, but it can do nothing to help constitute his human selfhood. The brightness in the triptych, the white garment, indicates that every human being is attracted by something outside himself that lures him out of his dark little chamber, whether it be a voice, or the words of an ideology, or other people's knowledge. But in order to become his own master, his own knowledge, and his own voice, he must divest himself of this outward manifestation of something not his own.

The direct relationship that has always existed between knowledge and liberty, on one had, and the idea of light and brightness, on the other, is shown by a further comparison between the triptych and another work. The contrast is provided this time by a May Day postcard issued by the German Social Democrats towards the end of the nineteenth century (p. 42). In the centre, we see members of the working population pressing forward, from left to right, towards an enthroned figure, the personification of Liberty. With hands outstretched, they receive from her hand the "Sword of the Spirit" that will give them freedom through knowledge. This is the message of the motto, "Knowledge is Power", that blazes forth from its hilt like a halo. What that knowledge rests on can be clearly seen beneath bright Liberty's right sandal: the writings of Marx, Darwin and Lassalle.

As far as the movement from darkness into light is concerned, this image shows a clear parallel to CLASS WAR. In both, human beings characterized by dark tones move from left to right in pursuit of a bright light. There is a conspicuous tendency to equate lightness with Above (see the background of CLASS WAR). The "enlightened" knowledge of the authors, Marx, Darwin and Lassalle, is not on the same plane as the marching human beings. On the contrary: Liberty with all her attributes is enthroned above them. The knowledge of liberty, and liberty itself, is thus equated with a being of a higher order, to whom men humbly aspire to rise. Both parties still bear the signs of the relationship between receiver and giver, servant and ruler. The knowledge of power, the sole guarantee of Liberty, is not that of lowly humanity but of someone else: and the image shows us that this someone is a person of superior status.

The postcard associates "light" with a specific body of knowledge, namely literature in the tradition of the Enlightenment; but there is nothing analogous to this in CLASS WAR and GATEWAY. Here, "light" takes the form of a light-coloured garment: a much more generalized statement.

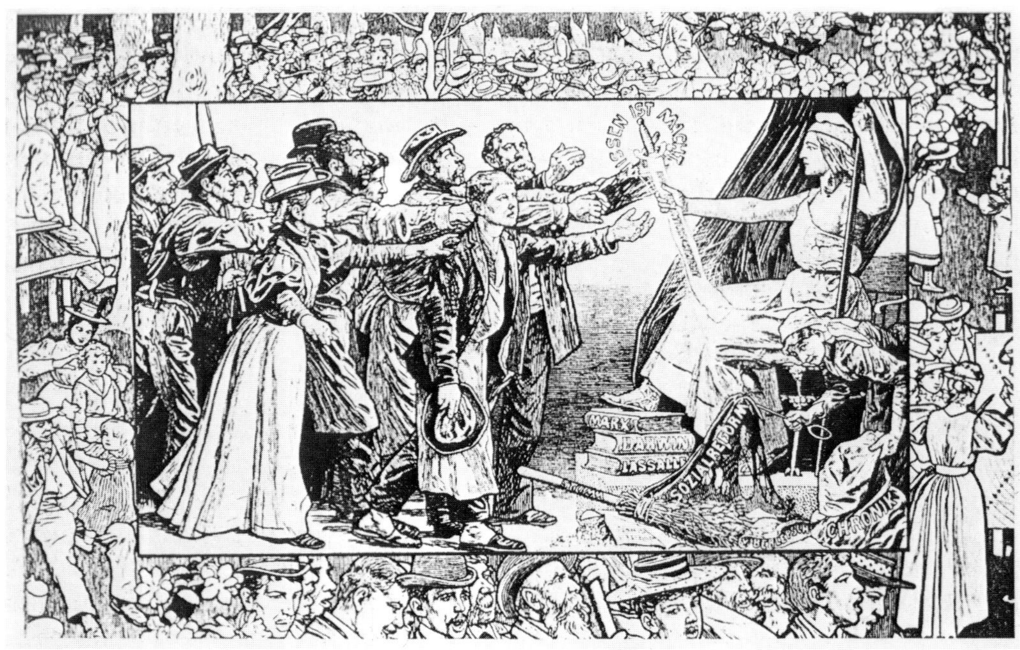

A May Day postcard of the german social democratic party, end of 19th century.

What counts here is simply that human beings are being drawn into the spell of a knowledge that is not theirs. In MILITANT, by contrast, the new and thus "dark" conception of light takes on a concrete and individual form. Precisely because the individual himself represents light, knowledge and liberty, he can be depicted in detail as a person. As the light tones did before them, the dark tones here represent truth, knowledge and liberty; except in this case all three of these qualities have to be generated by the individual.

This reversal of values does not negate light as the goal of the path of purification but redefines it. The supreme being, the Light of the World, is man as he constitutes his physical self, from which he derives his own individual knowledge. To be the Light is to form one's personal existence through self-acceptance, rather than found it on other people's opinions or forms of knowledge. It means using one's own body in all its complexity as a source of individual knowledge and action, and abandoning all supposedly higher and dominant criteria of validity in favour of one's own.

The statement at the beginning of this essay, that Gilbert & George's triptych is equivalent to a traditional initiatory progression, through the depths of darkness and on to rebirth, now appears to have been reversed. For the darkness – the Hell, as it were – through which the young human being passes is none other than the illusory promise of liberty, offered to him in the guise of light by knowledge not his own. But this extraneous light – this symbol of the snares and temptations of other people's knowledge – is darkness all over again, because it deceives him and leads him astray.

SPACE AND TIME

Light distribution and plant motifs define the theme of the triptych; the background represents the place where it all happens. It picks up motifs from the foreground and repeats their general outlines. In CLASS WAR, the background repeats the theme of the procession of human beings; in MILITANT, it echoes the respective directions of the branches and of their thorns. In addition to these reciprocal relationships, the background simultaneously serves to define the space in which the scene as a whole takes place. It localizes the process of human self-constitution, the donning and doffing of the white garment, and the emergence of the upright, autonomous individual: all take place within the city. Man's world, his environment, is modern city life. This is another link with the Last Judgment motif, which promised the elect not a rural existence but the delights of life within the walls of the Heavenly Jerusalem (p. 35).

It is not only the streets and buildings in this triptych that allude to space. Foreground and background combine to supply a visual conception and definition of space by announcing a number of spatial coordinates. The fourfold presentation of a given motif, shared by CLASS WAR and MILITANT, falls within this context. The background motif of CLASS WAR appears four times; and at the head of the procession stand four young men, the same number of figures as fill the image in MILITANT. Four is clearly a favoured number in this triptych, and this is because it corresponds to the coordinates of space: north, south, east, west; or front, back, left, right. To show a motif four times over is to define the spatial coordinates: to indicate where space operates, where it aligns and where it manifests itself.

The four cardinal points, which in this case are the four directions of urban space, as symbolically conveyed in the triptych by the location and the protagonists of the action, serve in all three pictures to reinforce the overall composition. This is particularly emphasized by the pronounced horizontal emphasis of the individual motifs and of the work as a whole. The spatial coordinates do not point up or down but across; and, similarly, a number of the motifs adopt a horizontal position in relation to the picture as a whole. This is conspicuous in MILITANT, where the branches are displaced out of their natural, vertical direction of growth to lie sideways. As well as figure groups and plant motifs, all four pictures share horizontal titles. The title of CLASS WAR, in particular, which projects to left and right beyond the signature below it, further emphasizes the horizontal position. The metaphoric use of light, outlined above, carries the same suggestion. The light here is not a heavenly but an earthly one, and it accordingly operates on earth.

This last feature of light, its earthbound action, is expressed by the leaf in CLASS WAR. By presenting itself as a circular form, unfolding in all directions at once, this once more reinforces the universality of the four coordinates of direction. These reduce all possible alignments of horizontal space to four basic vectors; and the leaf, like a circular line, shows them all. Four coordinates define the axial cross of space; the circle denotes space as fullness. The leaf, as a natural organism, marks the quality, the dynamic, of centrifugal movements within that space. Clearly, the leaf has nothing to do with the mathematically or geometrically defined space of a physics based on logical argument. Its space is physical in a highly organic sense. The many drops of water on the surface of the leaf denote the process of proliferating, sustaining growth that extends into the horizontal space of the city. The directions of space, and all that move within it, are to grow and fill with life.

In all the themes so far described within the triptych, the central focus is on the growth and formation of life: in man, both as an individual and as a social being; in plant life; and in man's urban environment. A "flowing" concept of space – one that symbolizes the growth of space through moisture, water, flourishing substance – is by no means unique to this triptych but, like others of its motifs, exists on an intercultural level. This may be illustrated by an example from the culture of the Navajo. Here the four cardinal points are symbolized, according to context and purpose, either by male or by female figures. If the latter, they are four women who are said to dwell in the "House of the Dewdrops" (p. 45).[6] To associate spatial coordinates with water, moisture and coolness, in order to promote growth, thus seems to be a widespread human concern. It represents the wish that human space may become fruitful. The four rivers that flow out from the

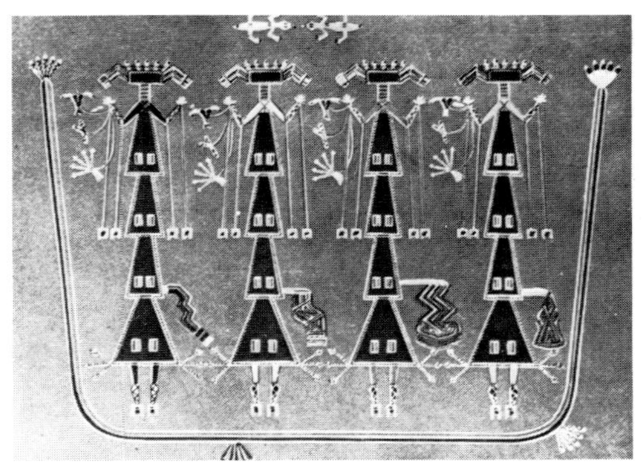

Four figures symbolizing the four directions are living in the "house of the dewdrops". Coloured flour drawing by the Navaho Indians.

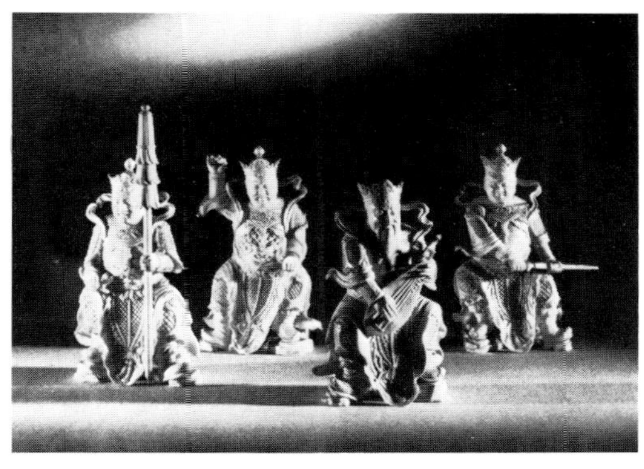

The four guardsmen of the world, China, Museum für Völkerkunde, Vienna.

centre of Paradise towards the four cardinal points belong to the same context (p. 47).

One small exception to the overall spatial structure of the triptych is afforded by GATEWAY. It shows a view of the same space, the city; and all three dominant motifs (man, plant, city) follow a marked horizontal orientation; but there is no allusion to the four cardinal points. Their absence is a consequence of the theme: the gateway is not the intersection of four paths but a place through which people pass in and out. The gateway represents a portal, a borderline, a threshold, that leads from one space into another; which is to say from CLASS WAR into MILITANT. This entry and exit process finds visual expression in GATEWAY in the way in which some of the young men are walking between the legs of the artists as if through a gate.

Like the other themes in the triptych, that of transition from one space into another, symbolized in GATEWAY, has an intercultural – and thus a general human – context. The building of a space defined by four coordinates, and the access to that space through a gateway or several gateways, makes its appearance not only in the cultural history of Europe but in that of several other continents. Religious buildings, above all – churches, temples, shrines – are defined by a direct connection between an entrance and a space based on a cruciform plan (p. 49).

Aside from this central significance, the number four has other applications in the religious context. Just as the four cardinal directions divide the heavens, the number four applies to other cosmic coordinates: it is used to order not only spaces and architecture but also doctrines, historical epochs, and human value systems: Four Ages of the World, Four Evangelists, Four Elements, Four Seasons, Four Cardinal Virtues. Although this is not repeated in every culture, it is frequently the case that a cosmic structure, an image of the cosmos, is defined in every aspect through the number four (p. 47). When further refined, this becomes eight, as the intermediate directions too are taken into consideration.

In Western culture, the connection between a space built up on four coordinates and a gateway that affords access to that space is most conspicuously represented in church architecture. A nave and transepts create the sacred space to which the portal admits the congregation. Through the portal – the gateway – the worshipper passes from profane space to a sacred space, defined by the cruciform plan, which extends to east, west, south, and north. Moreover, the portal has other functions besides that of an entrance. It gives instruction to the worshipper, through images, on selected biblical themes; it teaches and edifies him; perhaps it shows him a concrete representation of the torments of Hell and the joys of Heaven. It is flanked by extensive iconographic programmes to prepare him for the place of Christian teaching that lies within; other motifs, mostly of animals, adopt a guarding, protecting posture. Lions or demons defend the sacred space and protect it from evil influences (p. 48).

Another example, this time from India, reveals a similar concept of space: the building of a stupa, the sacred building form of Buddhist and Jain religion (p. 49/50). The one illustrated here consists of a cylindrical base surmounted first by a dome and then by an umbrella-like baldachin. This centrally planned structure has four entrances, all emphasized by large free-standing gateways symmetrically placed to face the cardinal points. The stupa is an image of the cosmos (dome), of its four cardinal directions (gateways) and of the heavens (baldachin). Like a church, it affords entry to a sacred space through a portal (in this case, four portals). Apart from their directional function, these portals also act as significant thresholds. Outside them lies the unordered world; within them, the microcosmic image of an intelligible macrocosm.

Gilbert & George's triptych shares with the church and the stupa a single spatial conception: that of an entrance followed by a space that allows movement in all directions in a horizontal plane. In each, the gateway signifies the transition to a state of salvation – whether divine or human. The triptych and the church differ notably in the way in which the church creates an additional separation between sacred and profane space. The triptych rejects this distinction between the earthly and the divine as

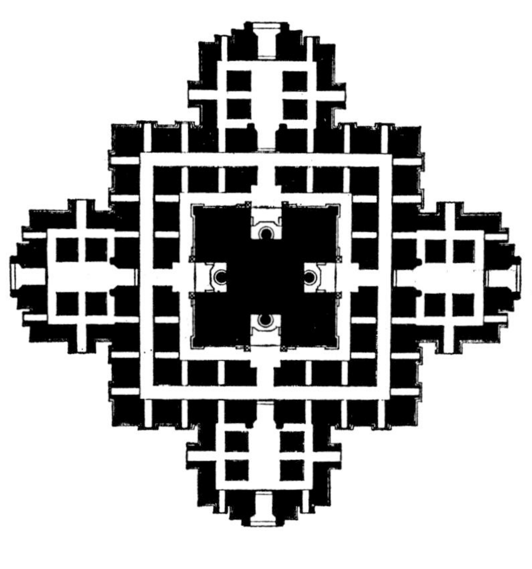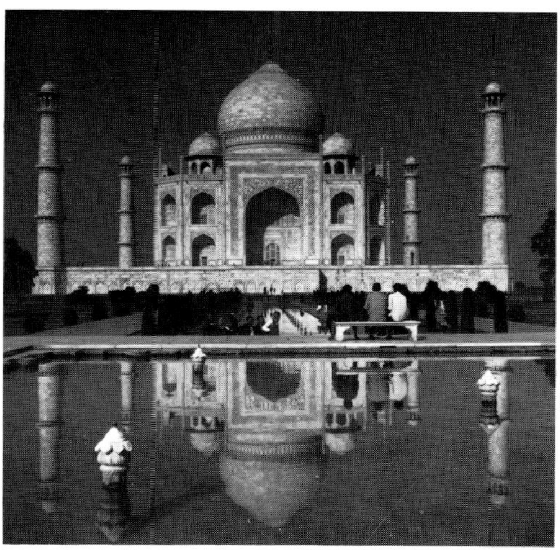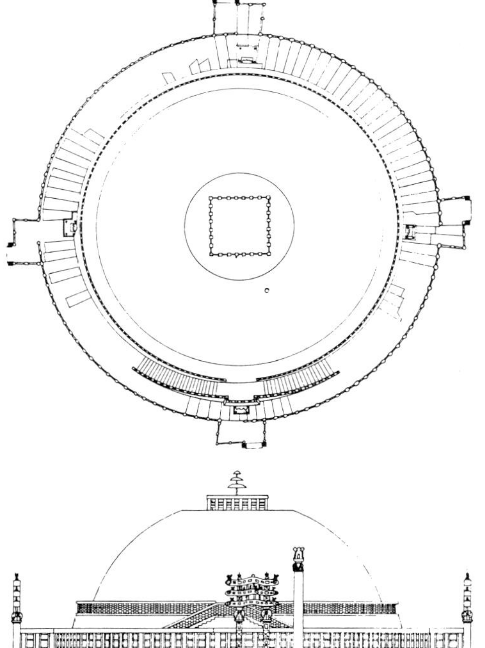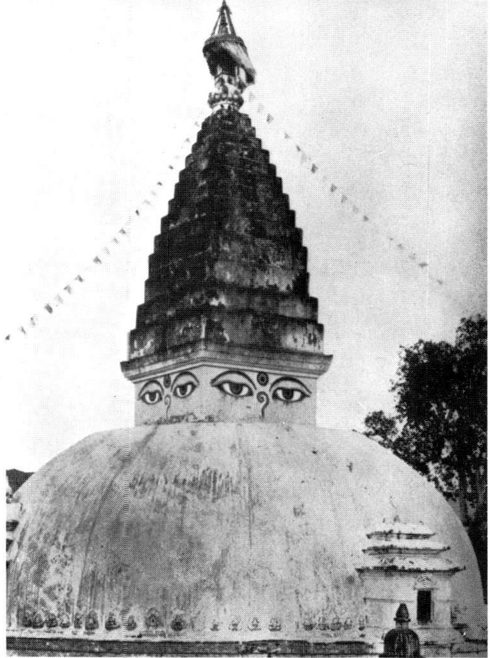

Architecture which is built up on a cross ground-plan. From left to right, top: Ground-plan of the Ananda Temple in Pagan (Birma), 1090; the Taj Mahal in Agra (India); bottom: Ground-plan and side-view of the stupa in Sanchi, India, (s. also following page); the stupa Carumati in Chabahil, Nepal.

49

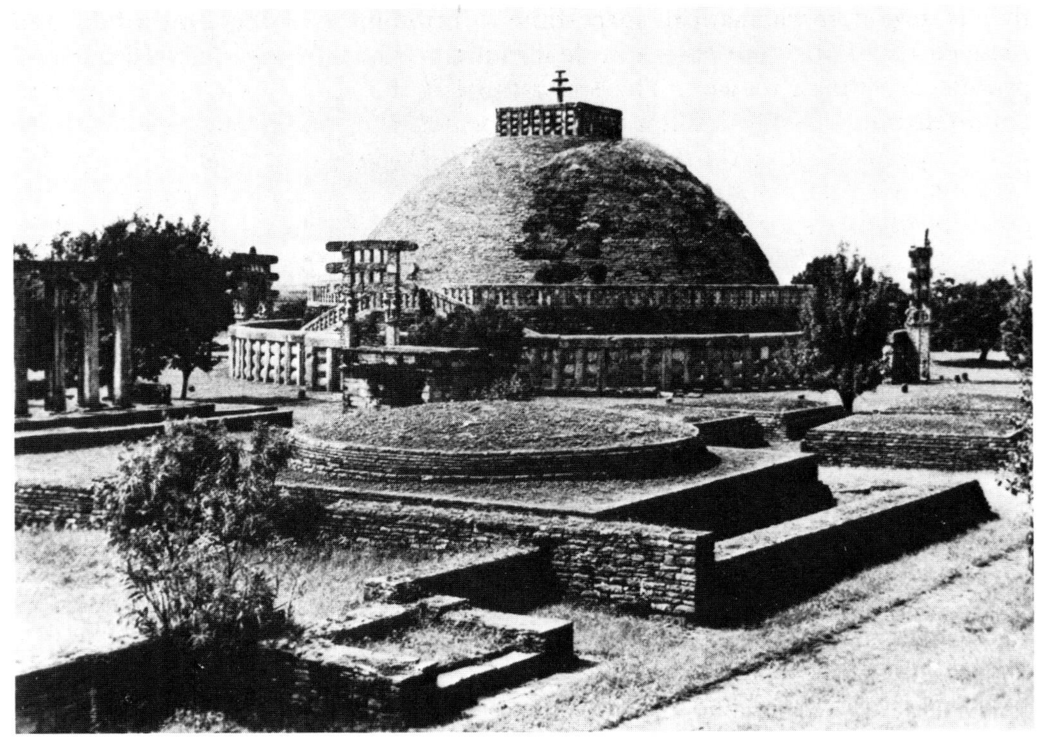

The stupa of Sanchi (India); see also preceding page.

firmly in its form as it does in its symbolic use of light. GATEWAY marks a threshold, all right, but not a threshold between the holy and the unholy, between the mundane and the transcendental. The two spaces between which the threshold of GATEWAY lies – the space of CLASS WAR and the space of MILITANT – are identically defined by the human environment, the city. GATEWAY simply separates the time before self-constitution from the time after it. Before GATEWAY, in CLASS WAR, man approaches that self-constitution; after GATEWAY, in MILITANT, man has attained it and is defending it. The passing of the threshold makes it possible for him to constitute himself as a body of light.

The conception of space in the triptych logically entails a conception of time. Without time, the space presented here would be unthinkable. Space contains time – just as, conversely, time gives birth to space. The human beings in all three pictures walk and move with time, their time; and that time in turn creates space. Time and space relate directly to each other. CLASS WAR represents a path, GATEWAY a threshold, MILITANT a stance; all three taken together form a spatiotemporal entity. But, again, this is not a mathematical space-time continuum – space objectified and reduced to an absolute common denominator – but a reciprocal relationship produced by man himself. The space-time of the scientists is an attempt to comprehend rational constants that operate as a universal law without human participation; the triptych effects a relationship created by man for his own benefit. Human beings themselves are the protagonists and the creators of this space-time. It begins and ends with them: this is the space and the time of their history. Hence also the red-green colour symbolism of the triptych. Green symbolizes osmotic growth; red marks as a signal the stages and the means of that growth: fruit, flower, and thorns, together with their common stem, the staff. Additionally, red emphasizes the line of sight, the direction of march, in the class war.

LOOKING FROM

BOURGEOISIE AND PROLETARIAT

So much for the analysis of the triptych. Its central panel and its wings yield an overall view of a class war that serves to promote the self-constitution of man. Above all, this class war is localized inside a cosmic structure with every class warrior as a part of its architecture. Or – conversely – the class war itself, together with all who participate in it, governs the erection of a human cosmic architecture that assigns to the individual a place, a time, and a relative position of his own. Contained within this class war is its goal: it holds out the prospect that liberty may be attained, not through a battle against any adversary, but through the constitution of a living architecture, made up of all human beings, and created at the joint behest of the individual and the community.

To clarify the political dimension of this constituent act, it is worth making a comparison with the class war as described at the outset: the class war according to Marx and Engels, as deduced from their analysis of history and written down in the Communist Manifesto. This has forfeited some of its topicality with the passage of time, but even so it represents a position from which to define Gilbert & George's triptych in still more concrete terms. Some statements by Marx and Engels, which have lost substance in relation to their own class war, take on a new truth in relation to the class war as newly formulated by Gilbert & George.

The class war in the triptych differs most notably from that described by Marx and Engels by virtue of the fact that there are no classes in it. The authors of the Communist Manifesto saw the class war as requiring the existence of at least two hostile classes; but in the work by Gilbert & George there is only one class. No class adversary, no class enemy, no oppressor is anywhere to be found; the most that there is to confront is an illusion. In terms of historical class conflict, all this looks like a paradox, a contradiction in terms: for the eventual disappearenance of classes is supposed to mark the end of the class war. When all men are equal at last, and no form of oppression separates them, then there is only one class left, namely the proletariat. A war within that single class would be a contradiction in terms, as no one in it is oppressing anyone else.

However, the class war, as Gilbert & George present it, is not about confrontation but about human fellowship. The artists here entirely redirect the class war concept. Instead of applying it reflectively to the past, they reformulate it with a view to the future. This is possible because their class war opens with the very state of affairs that for Marx and Engels represented the end of theirs: the attainment of equality between individuals. The authors of the Communist Manifesto saw the class war within the context of a social pyramid, in which the upper class rules the lower (p. 53). The class war as conceived by Gilbert & George exists within a society of equal individuals. This is yet another reason for the horizontal orientation of their triptych: all are on the same level, and there are no distinctions between oppressors and oppressed, no ideological rift between base and superstructure.

The triptych thus denies the existence of a class enemy who might stand in the way of the human quest for a liberated life. It is here that Gilbert & George are responding to present-day circumstances: for it is only with great effort that these can be made to yield the traditional pattern of class hostility. However defined, the image of a class enemy has begun

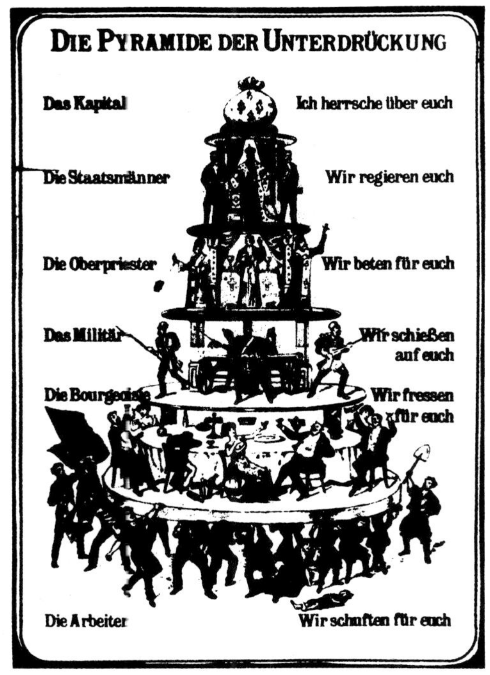

The pyramid of oppression, 19th century.

to crumble; it has lost potency, and is kept alive only by the continuing belief in its existence. Some remnants of the old system of oppression may persist, but they are no longer worth fighting. A much more rewarding struggle is the new class war, in which society and individuals pursue their own path. The pairs of eyes in CLASS WAR symbolize this process. They stare straight ahead, concentrating on their objective, and need no longer focus on traditional enemies. The war that is in progress here is such as to suggest that we eliminate the old adversaries by consistently ignoring them and by following our own path. Even to glance at them would only strengthen them and prolong their imaginary existence; to look straight along one's own path makes them disappear. A strategic concept.

The new class war differs from the old only in the lack of any "oppressive power" in the triptych but in the identity of the participants. This is most clearly evident if we look at the combatants in the former class war. Marx and Engels spoke of a conflict between the bourgeoisie, "owners of the means of social production", and the proletariat, "the class of modern wage-labourers ... reduced to selling their labour-power" to the former as a commodity. Between the two there existed a relationship of total dependency that caused the proletariat to grow constantly larger and also poorer, while the ruling class grew ever richer and more powerful. In particular, the absorption of traditional areas of work into machine production, the disappearance of independent crafts and the accumulation of capital in a few hands meant that merchants, craftsmen, peasant farmers and small industrialists sank into the proletariat. This was the state of affairs that led Marx and Engels to conclude: "Thus the proletariat is recruited from all classes of the population."[7] They regarded the proletariat as an international phenomenon, applicable to every section of society.

The triptych might appear to display no trace of the existence of these two classes. But both are nevertheless represented by their most notable and conspicuous features. The participants in the class war here initially remind us of the proletariat as described by Marx and Engels. They too are recruited from all "classes" of the population: not only that, but from differing cultures. But since their social origins do not show either in their clothing or in any other characteristics, they correspond to the proletariat as described by Marx and Engels after it has formed itself, from the most varied sections of the population, into a class of equals. Their fathers may have been worlds apart, but the sons are united on a single level.

Although all the figures in the triptych thus belong to the proletariat, they simultaneously present themselves as representatives of the opposite party, the bourgeoisie. The persons shown here have abolished the antithesis between the oppressors and the oppressed by elevating themselves, in their own capacity as proletarians, into the bourgeoisie. This is confirmed by the staves in CLASS WAR and MILITANT. These are not only symbols of erectness and defence but for that very reason also symbols of the means to those ends: the autonomous productivity and strength of the individual. The staves are a sign that everyone is his own master and the source of his own mastery, which – because he is a proletarian – he does not use to rule or to oppress others. This is one reason for the absence of the traditional class enemy in the triptych: both parties have become one. The class of proletarians constitutes itself by using means and weapons derived from the bourgeoisie. The prophecy in the Communist Manifesto is thus fulfilled, not through the death of the bourgeoisie but through its resurrection as a proletarian fellowship: "But not only has the bourgeoisie forged the weapons that bring death to itself; it has also called into existence the men who are to wield those weapons – the modern working class – the proletarians."[8]

DEMOCRACY

The rise of the proletariat to become the ruling class was of course a general aspiration long before Gilbert & George made their triptych. It first emerged long ago in the central Communist slogan of the "dictatorship of the proletariat". But in the form of this dictatorship, in the manner of government and control, in the principle of dominance, the two conceptions are far apart; and the distinction consists in the relationship between the individual and society.

What did the Communist Manifesto predict, once the state of proletarian dictatorship was attained and the bourgeoisie dethroned? Essentially, the destinies of the Communist country were to be directed by a centralized state power, superior to the individual, that would take possession of all those means to the acquisition of power that had formerly been owned by the bourgeoisie. This state power would represent the will of the proletariat, and would thus be a democratic government that would guarantee the liberties of a free society precisely by virtue of its organized centralization of power. The idea was this: in order to eliminate any possibility of oppression and exploitation, means were to be withdrawn from individuals and handed over to the state. To describe this situation – in which people who have no means live in a state that is rich in means – Marx and Engels use the term "association". At the end of the second section of the Communist Manifesto this word takes on a utopian colouring: "In place of the old bourgeois society, with its classes and class antagonisms, we shall have an association, in which the free development of each is the condition for the free development of all."[9]

Today, after decades of Communist regimes, the utopian model of the state postulated by Marx and Engels has been seen in action. In place of an "association" that guarantees and fosters liberty, there is a ruling state apparatus using all the oppressive mechanisms of a totalitarian regime. However, this represents only one of the most extreme verisons of the postulated relationship between individual and society. Nor is there anything exclusively "Communist" about this relationship. For any state model that seeks to regulate individual freedom and collective will, whether in a Communist or a non-Communist society, is fundamentally tied to a traditional and dualistic system of government. This entails the existence of a single ruling body, to which the individuals are subordinate. In the Communist model of society this is represented by the state, with its wealth of resources: the central power that individuals have organized. The role of the former rulers is taken over by a principle that purports to have been democratically established by all. Although in theory this principle has been devised and instituted by an association of equals, it is really the old principle of dominance: one single authority for all. Instead of everyone being permitted to govern himself, a higher and ostensibly general and objective will is to govern everyone. This is a dualistic system of rule.

Why does Communism, which on the face of it is an anti-hierarchic ideology, thus uncritically accept the old system of rule? The answer lies in the fear that lies profoundly embedded in its conception of the nature of rule itself. Communism has never been able to conceive of rule except in terms of domination – the oppression of others, never the self-determination achieved by an individual who is free of all dependence on his fellow human beings. Rule, as the Communist Manifesto saw it in historical retrospect, had always meant two things: first, a centre of power, from which rule emanated; second, the persons dependent on that power centre. Rule in this sense emerges from the traditional conception of the relationship between God and man, whereby God directed, guided and judged human beings, and they were dependent on him in everything they did. Whether secular or ecclesiastical, feudal or bourgeois, and earthly governing entity was always there to imitate God's universal rule by wielding the sceptre beneath which the mass of the governed – subject, dependent, productive – lived their lives.

In full awareness of this, the Communist Manifesto proceeded to reproduce exactly the same form of rule. Its authors imagined that they had obviated any such catastrophic error by abolishing class distinctions; but they failed to see that the dictatorship of the proletariat would infallibly reproduce the familiar model of rule with all its omnipotence and its division into Above and Below. For within the class of the proletariat no one was to build his own life free of restraint: the lives of all would be articulated, structured, formed and directed by a supposedly proletarian, unitary, universal will. The idea that the proletariat was united not only by the equality that exists among its members but by the desire for a single, unified pattern of economic and social relations and social organization, went so deep that the old principle of rule was automatically, if unavowedly, perpetuated. The belief in a general principle superior to all individuals, and in a state organization manned by the proletariat that would regularly intervene in the individual's life on the pretext of furthering his well-being, reflects the old form of rule with its Above and Below, its relationship between the one who wields the sceptre and the one who takes orders.

Before this old relationship between society and individual can be compared and contrasted with the state of affairs in Gilbert & George's triptych, it is worth looking at one of the artists' earlier works, THE QUEUE (p. 58). The upper third of the picture shows a line of people standing one behind the other, as in CLASS WAR; in the centre, as in MILITANT, individuals are shown frontally. The work centres on collectivity and individuality. The triptych, in its three separate panels, does something comparable – with the immediately apparent difference that its protagonists hold in their hands a means to an end, namely their staves. The people in THE QUEUE stand in public space: democratically, because all are equal in status, but inactively. In the triptych they take their destinies into their own hands. This distinction leads to the new relationship between individual and society.

What is general and what is individual in this triptych? One thing that is general – alongside the fact that the theme itself is general, as can be seen from the everyday scene in the background of CLASS WAR – is the staff, an implement accessible to all, a proletarian and democratic version of the sceptre. This, or its multiple, embodies the universal factor that constitutes the general consensus. Everyone can take it up, and everyone can use it for his own purposes. What is "individual" in this context is the act of taking up this generally recognized and universal instrument of self-rule and giving it one's own uniquely personal form. CLASS WAR shows the universal principle; MILITANT shows the individual's part in it.

The triptych, in its presentation of the relationship between individual and society – as in its metaphorical use of light and in its interpretation of the concept of space – utterly negates the existence of a principle superior

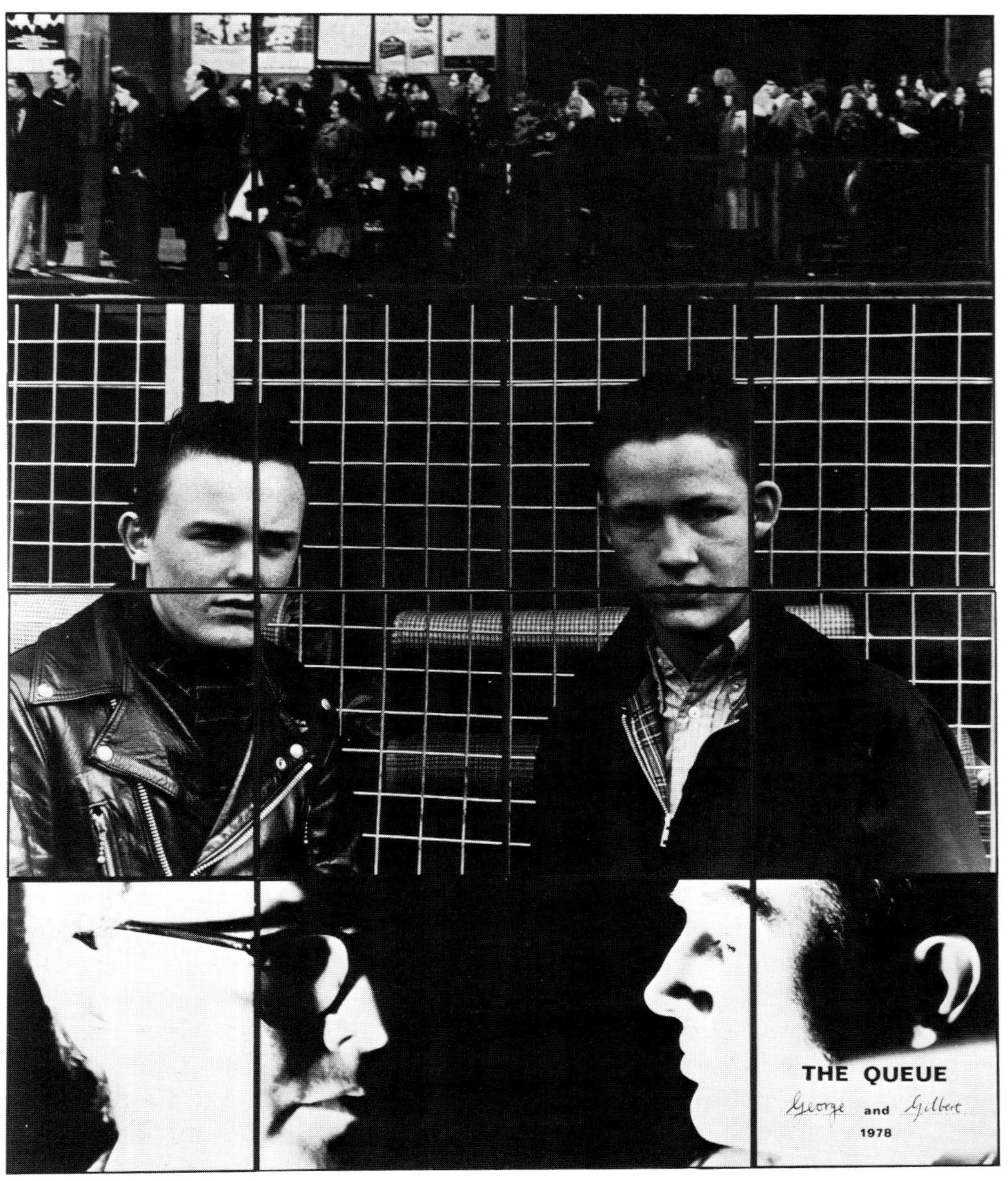

THE QUEUE, 1978, 241 x 201 cm.

to man. Under the old hierarchical relationship, the right to rule was removed from the individual and assigned to an all-embracing and – at best – democratically controlled principle; the triptych looks another form of democracy straight in the eye. Democracy here does not mean the democratically delegated will of a people, to which all must yield, but on the contrary society's general will that each individual must deploy his own will to the utmost. All are equal, and thus immune to the danger of wanting to control their neighbours. The concord among these people manifest itself in their respect for each other's autonomy. All rule, because none dominates any other, and because no one's individual self-rule stands in any need of a democratic check. In morality, ethics, work, commerce, and social life, everyone is his own master. At the same time, this also frees him from the customary delegation of responsibility. Where no superior authority any longer organizes his life for him, he and he alone is responsible.

Where previously the individual's life was governed by a generally applicable principle derived from the public domain, in the triptych that same public domain is defined through individual acts of self-constitution. The previous relationship between the individual and society is reversed. Society no longer consists of a web, a network, pulling men's actions together; its organization now consists in the sum of numerous individual and mutually independent agents. In place of a single, universally applicable Nature, setting its stamp on individual lives, society presents a many-sided spectacle defined by its numerous, varied and individual component units. Nor does this mean a horde of autonomous but isolated individuals; this is clear from MILITANT, which is the image of the goal of self-constitution. By dividing its plant motif, the thorny branch, in the centre, and assigning each half to a pair of human beings, it makes this coherence visible. The individuals are not joined by a single stem, forcibly holding them together: a number of stems yield a number of viable and mutually independent units.

The society that the triptych postulates, both in collective and individual terms, is one that has often been invoked in the past: a society without classes, and without a state. It is, in fact, both class and state in one; and its founding principle, its overriding and sovereign idea, is the freedom of the individual to constitute himself; it thus renders the old concepts of state and class redundant. There is neither state nor class, in the sense of a superior authority regulating the individual's life. Nor is there a state, claiming a monopoly of power and operating through a limited number of state institutions. The power of the state is exercised by every individual for himself, and by all acting together to enforce individual freedom. To adapt the sentence by Marx and Engels quoted above, it may be said of the triptych that: "In place of the old bourgeois society, with its classes and class antagonisms, we shall have an autonomous governing principle; and this, as the free development of each, will condition the free development of all."

A DEMOCRATIC LANGUAGE

In the light of their historical analysis, the authors of the Communist Manifesto saw the future of society primarily in international terms. Because the bourgeoisie, identified by them as the class in power, operated world-wide and was still expanding, it followed that the phenomenon of a constantly multiplying proletariat must also manifest itself globally. Their prophetic vision of a Communist society was not a national solution but one founded in a world-wide view. The slogan "Working men of all countries, unite!" is evidence of this. Communism was to rule everywhere.

The internationalism of class war is present in Gilbert & George's triptych as it is in the Communist Manifesto; the distinction between the two is precisely as defined above. Thus, in the triptych, the combatants still wage class war, indeed on an international level; but they themselves form a synthesis of proletariat and bourgeoisie. This is in contrast to the Communist pattern, where they would have belonged exclusively to the proletariat while accepting the power structures of the bourgeoisie in the form of an impersonal state authority. Internationalism is common to both formulas; what distinguishes them is individual self-determination.

It is not only the figures in the triptych who define it as international. The language that Gilbert & George use has global aspects of its own: as in the theme, common to all three pictures, of human self-constitution as a process of evolution from darkness to light. As explained at the outset, not only is this theme intercultural, because universally human: it is entirely ahistorical, because it actually embodies history. Or, to put it another way: it transcends history, because it represents a universal rather than a particular historical phenomenon. The same goes for the staff motif and the conception of space; so that as a whole and in detail the triptych refers neither to a specific time nor to a specific place. It locates the class war in the places where modern civilization resides: in the cities, and thus worldwide.

Apart from the international cast of figures and the intercultural, because universally human, theme, the internationalism of the triptych has a further linguistic aspect: anyone can read the work without any prior knowledge. Gilbert & George rely on no specific or locally explicable form of the motifs involved; nor does any partial aspect of the work stand in any need of historical explanation. All the motifs are to be found, variously characterized, throughout time and space; and yet the triptych can be understood without benefit of historical memory. The metaphorical use of light, the play of light and dark, the configuration of space with the aid of four cardinal directions, its quality as urban terrain, the natural symbolism of plant life: to understand any of these things requires no prior knowledge. The meaning expresses itself on the surface of things, and not – either in time or in space – behind them.

The triptych as a whole is consistently democratic. Anyone can participate, anyone can read, and anyone can join in erecting the new democracy that is imaged here, by first constituting his own selfhood. His image is a component of the overall picture. What the individual can no longer do, however, is appeal to any higher authority. There is no party, no state apparatus, no government, no ideology, no employer, no scapegoat of any sort, to blame for the inadequacies of our lives. Everyone is his own master, and so the responsibility, in all matters, rests with him.

This picture of a new democracy, which summons the individual to maintain collective human life, responds to a present situation by opening up new perspectives. Hitherto, democracy has defined itself as an attempt to break down the power structures of a previously hierarchically ordered society. But what is to happen when all ranks are levelled, all the mechanisms of oppression removed? Is some state administration to hold the fate of individuals in its hands; or are individuals to decide their own fate? If the latter offers a way forward, this can no longer represent a liberation from putative external forces, but the constitution of a personal freedom: not freedom as a form of "being set free", but freedom as a form of evolution, of unfolding.

LIBERTY AND RULE

When Marx and Engels published their Communist Manifesto, they drew a line beneath all previous history. They saw that this had been a history of conflicts waged by differing classes, and that it was for the future to put an end to that conflict by insisting that mankind become a single, undifferentiated class. Also they recognized that such differences and conflicts had always hitherto been the result of an inequitable distribution of means. One class possessed and ruled, and the other was dependent on it. This led to wars and revolutions: "an uninterrupted ... fight that each time ended, either in a revolutionary reconstitution of society at large, or in the common ruin of the contending classes" (quoted above).

Seen from this perspective, two things can be understood and readily appreciated: first, that Marx and Engels expected to see class war disappear as the result of the total dominance of one class, the proletariat; and second, that they sought to entrust the distribution of power and of the means of production, hitherto so unjustly organized, to a state authority set up by the proletariat. The institution of this state monopoly of power and property was based on the historical insight that in private hands these must inevitably lead to personal relationship of dependency. Because, in the past, rule had always meant some people dominating others, the authors found no alternative but to entrust that rule to a public authority distinct from any individual.

It is in relation to the image of rule, particularly, that Gilbert & George's triptych seeks to move in a completely different direction. Rule as the domination and enslavement of others, as abuse of power, as an authority constantly requiring public scrutiny, or as a universally binding system, is absent. Rule here entails neither omnipotence nor circumscribed freedom of action. Rule shows itself in the three pictures as a democratic means to a personal end, available to all. Perhaps it is the plant element here that best indicates the divergence from the traditional hierarchical relationship: it characterizes the emerging form of rule as a physical, biological process, leading every being to unfold and attain his autonomy, rather than as a cancerous growth that threatens to overwhelm and stifle all others.

With this image of a new and democratic form of rule, Gilbert & George associate the classless humanity invoked by Marx and Engels. But here they place power and rule in the hands of individuals – which is precisely where Marx and Engels, with their traditional conception of rule and authority, never intended them to be. This is one reason why the class war, which in the classless society was expected to become a thing of the past, is here unleashed all over again. No longer is the class to fight against an adversary but for itself. Now that the class warriors hold in their hands a newly formulated, and in particular a human, form of power, it is they alone who daily reassert their own existence and their own liberty. They wage the war by committing their strength to the constitution of their own selfhood.

Once given a new model of rule, the aspects of class war identified by Marx and Engels in their study of history remain no less valid today. Their statement that "every class struggle is a political struggle"[10] applies perfectly to the new class war – as does the idea, already quoted, of a "revolutionary reconstitution of society at large". Even where Marx and Engels, speaking

of a succession of competing classes, explicitly identify the negative conse-
quences of class conflict, their verdict is transformed into a positive one as
soon as there is only one class. "All the preceding classes that got the upper
hand sought to fortify their already acquired status by subjecting society at
large to their conditions of appropriation."[11] Once all the members of society belong to a single class, this "subjection" is no longer a danger but on
the contrary an enrichment for all: it is the confirmation of a democratic
principle. All this is supported by the fact that – like those who waged the
historical class war – those who wage the new class war form the broad
and, in terms of the triptych, the horizontal basis of human existence: "The
proletarian movement is the self-conscious, independent movement of the
immense majority, in the interest of the immense majority."[12] This is just
what the triptych shows, with the addition that here the proletarian movement is simultaneously a bourgeois movement.

MONARCHY AS DEMOCRACY

There have been several references in this essay to the intercultural aspects
of the triptych. In themselves, these form an important departure from the
class war as formerly defined, which laid its stress on international rather
than cultural considerations. In fact, "intercultural" is by no means synony-
mous with "international", even though the two terms are not mutually
exclusive. "Intercultural" refers primarily to the detection of a pattern that
is to be found in all cultures and consequently represents something universal to humanity. What do the intercultural components of the triptych
amount to? No more and no less than the image and the constitution of a
kingdom. This may initially seem disconcerting in view of previous statements concerning the democratic nature of Gilbert & George's triptych.
But the Western supposition that monarchy and democracy represent
diametrically opposite forms of society is historically conditioned. It fails to
take into account that monarchy primarily signifies the creation of a human
centre, the erection of a human space, rather than the domination and
oppression of others.

The image of the king, his realm and his rule, are found in many
cultures, reduced to a few signs that call for symbolic interpretation. The
essentials of this symbolism, as discussed by Philipp Wolff-Windegg in his
book Die *Gekrönten*[13], are as follows. First there is man, interpreting his
own standpoint as the centre of the world. When he looks round, he

becomes aware of a circular horizon. Second, having thus defined himself as the centre of a circle, he proceeds to define that circle as his space, his world, and begins to divide it into four coordinates, which structure it and give it a profile. Third, at the centre of this world – of his own space – he plants his sceptre, the symbol of his rule and the sign of his own Tree of Life. Fourth, man at the centre of his world represents kingship and therefore light. He is the Light of the World.

All four criteria of kingship, as defined here, are to be found in the triptych. Man's space, his world, is formed here by the city, with its round horizon like the leaf in CLASS WAR. This is then divided in accordance with the four cardinal points. Man takes his place in the centre as the bearer of the sceptre: as the one who acts, directs, takes responsibility, creates his own kingdom and defends it. Finally, in MILITANT, man represents the king, the body of light. The distinction between this and all previous kingdoms is marked by the absence of any hierarchical structure, any gradient between Above and Below. Democracy, defined as space and freedom for individual action, and monarchy, defined as the constitution of that space and that freedom, form a perfect unity. No longer is one single person to rule. All can rule; for their rule requires no one to be the ruled or the oppressed.

The triptych also reveals another intercultural pattern of monarchic liberation. The path from darkness to light, the Path of Kings, is an initiatory journey, such as is found in many cultures. In this case, however, the darkness through which man must pass is represented by the brightness that lures and beckons him into regions that to him are dim and obscure. The light-coloured garment is none other than a symbol for man's confinement by powers alien and external to himself: powers that may indeed be figments of his imagination. It is a sign of man's tendency to take his bearings from something other than himself, whether it be the concept of some superior being or the opinions and actions of others. Once he has cast this orientation aside like an old garment, he begins to unfold his own freedom. Democracy here demands of everyone the active principle of autonomous development and responsibility, the courage to set himself free from prevalent opinions, doctrines, precepts, and other directives.

These specifically monarchic demands are the clearest of the gulf between this conception and that of the traditional class war – or of its goal, the Communist society. That model still relied on the presence of the old monarch, a person who – even if invisible and incarnated only in an administrative structure – undertook to feed, protect and care for the people. No individual was to take the place of the king: instead, a faceless Party was to assume responsibility for a subject population while simultaneously telling it how to live. Gilbert & George's triptych, by contrast, is a call for a democratic society; it elevates the constitution of personal and monarchic selfhood into a democratic principle of life.

In our time a number of works of art have already become key works of the twentieth century. Gilbert & George's triptych might count as a key work of the transition from the twentieth century to the twenty-first. Not only because of its theme of threshold and transition, but above all because of its political nature. It presents political action as autonomous and individual action, and couples the place of politics once more with its point of origin: the *polis* through the image of the modern metropolis. What is more, it fills the vacuum created by the collapse of formerly dominant ideologies and their attendant utopias. It stands for a future that is again worth working for.

There are some direct conclusions to be drawn from the picture of the new class war and of its protagonists. What does it mean, aside from the image of a new democracy, if every human being becomes an autonomous ruler; if no superior authority, no higher being – whether Church, Central Committee, Party, Parliament, or Government – any longer limits his freedom of decision; in short, if he takes sole responsibility for his own existence in every respect? It means that here, for the very first time, man becomes the being whose creature he always imagined himself to be: namely, God.

It was not God who created man in his own image; man created God in his. There was always a God who knew no superior, a God who held sway in all things, a God who acted and created alone; but now man has assumed that role, with all that follows. The role always has been his, of course; but for too long his belief in superior powers lured him into a pursuit of the dazzling light of some imaginary, higher, metaphysical being, whether a God or a dominant form of knowledge.

The glory of the divine, however, belongs to man alone. Not in an apotheosis of man – as has tended to be assumed in earlier versions of the idea – but on the contrary, in a humanization of God. This, too, the triptych proposes. Man here remains entirely man, in his physical organism as in his immediate environment, the city. He is not liberated from earthly ties, nor does he soar aloft to higher spheres. He recognizes, in his deeply human nature, that he alone is the being in whose hands his fate, his freedom, and his knowledge lie. For this reason, the word "his" is to be applied not to God the Father but to man, in the words of the Lord's Prayer: for his is the kingdom, the power and the glory, for ever and ever

AMEN.

NOTES

1 Karl Marx and Friedrich Engels, The Communist Manifesto, tr. Samuel Moore (Hardmondsworth: Penguin Books, 1967 etc.), 79.
2 Ibid., 80.
3 Manfred Lurker (ed.), "Wörterbuch der Symbolik", Stuttgart 1988, 422.
4 Up until now, the triptychon has been shown in four places. 1987 in the Lenbachhaus, Munich, in the Hayward Gallery, London, in the Stedelijk Museum, Amsterdam, and 1991 in the exhibition METROPOLIS, Martin-Gropius-Bau, Berlin.
5 Gilbert & George first made use of the word "sculpture" at the beginning of their career, from about 1968 onwards, when they presented themselves as LIVING SCULPTURES. For their subsequent work, which is essentially two-dimensional, they have retained the same term. Sculpture, in this sense, does not refer to a genre based on modelling so much as to an independently valid, non-reflective artwork.
6 "Architektur der primitiven Kulturen", Stuttgart, 1975, 128–30. Germanic mythology likewise refers to the connection between architecture and water. It tells of the World Tree, Yggdrasil, over which a mead-like dew trickles to keep it alive for ever. Water thus serves to maintain the entire structure of the cosmos. See Pierre Grimal, Mythen der Völker, 3 (Frankfurt/Main, 1967): 54.
7 Marx and Engels (as note 1), 88.
8 Ibid., 87.
9 Ibid., 105.
10 Ibid., 90.
11 Ibid., 92.
12 Ibid., 92.
13 Philipp Wolff-Windegg, "Die Gekrönten", Stuttgart 1958, chapter 1 "Vom Wesen der Mitte", 21–24, and chapter 7 "Der Ort der Herrschaft".

EXHIBITIONS
(Selected – listed chronologically)

Solo Exhibitions – Galleries and Museums

1968	THREE WORKS – THREE WORKS	Frank's Sandwich Bar, London
1969	OUR NEW SCULPTURE	St. Martin's School of Art, London
1970 to 1973	UNDERNEATH THE ARCHES	among others in: Kunsthalle Düsseldorf; Museo d'Arte Moderna, Turin; Stadsbiblioteket Lyngby, Copenhagen; Heiner Friedrich Galerie, Cologne; National Gallery of New South Wales, John Kaldor Project, Sydney
1971	THE PAINTINGS	Stedelijk Museum, Amsterdam; Whitechapel Art Gallery, London; Kunstverein Düsseldorf
1971	THE GENERAL JUNGLE	Sonnabend Gallery, New York
1972	THE BAR	Anthony d'Offay Gallery, London
1973	THE SHRUBBERIES & SINGING SCULPTURE	National Gallery of New South Wales, John Kaldor Project, Sydney; National Gallery of Victoria, John Kaldor Project, Melbourne
1973	ANY PORT IN A STORM	Sonnabend Gallery, Paris
1974	DARK SHADOW	Art & Project, Amsterdam
1975	BLOODY LIFE	Galerie Lucio Amelio, Naples
1976	THE GENERAL JUNGLE	Albright-Knox Gallery, Buffalo
1977	RED MORNING	Sperone Fischer Gallery, Basle
1978	NEW PHOTO-PIECES	Art Agency, Tokyo
1980 1981	PHOTO-PIECES 1971–1980,	Stedelijk van Abbemuseum, Eindhoven; Kunsthalle Düsseldorf; Kunsthalle Bern; Centre national d'art et de Culture Georges Pompidou, Paris; Whitechapel Art Gallery, London
1981	PHOTO-PIECES 1980–1981	Crousel-Hussenot Gallery, Paris
1982	NEW PHOTO-PIECES	Gewad, Ghent
1983	PHOTO-PIECES 1980–1982	David Bellmann Gallery, Toronto
1984	HANDS UP	Gallery Schellmann & Klüser, Munich

1984 GILBERT & GEORGE   The Norton Gallery of Art, West Palm Beach, Florida;
1985   The Baltimore Museum of Art; Contemporary Arts
                                  Museum, Houston; Milwaukee Art Museum; The
                                  Solomon R. Guggenheim Museum, New York

1985 NEW MORAL WORKS   Sonnabend Gallery, New York

1986 PICTURES 1982 TO 1985   CAPC Musée d'Art contemporain, Bordeaux; Palais des
                                  Beaux-Arts, Brussels; Palacio Velázquez, Madrid;
                                  Lenbachhaus Munich; Hayward Gallery, London

1987 GILBERT & GEORGE   Aldrich Museum of Contemporary Art, Connecticut
      PICTURES

1989 THE 1988 PICTURES   Christian Stein Gallery, Milan

1989 FOR AIDS EXHIBITION   Anthony d'Offay Gallery, London

1990 GILBERT & GEORGE   New Tretyakow Gallery, Moscow
      PICTURES 1983–1988

1990 THE NEW COSMO-   Sonnabend Gallery, New York
      LOGICAL PICTURES

1990 WORLDS AND WINDOWS   Anthony d'Offay Gallery, London

Group Exhibitions

1969 CONCEPTION   Städtisches Museum, Leverkusen

1970 CONCEPTUAL ART, ARTE   Galleria Civica d'Arte Moderna, Turin
      POVERA, LAND ART

1970 (UNTITLED)   CAYC, Buenos Aires

1971 THE BRITISH   Cultural Center, New York
      AVANT-GARDE

1972 DOCUMENTA 5   Kassel

1973 FROM HENRY MOORE   Palais des Beaux-Arts, Brussels
      TO GILBERT & GEORGE

1974 KUNST BLEIBT KUNST   Kunsthalle Köln

1976 ARTE INGLESE OGGI   Palazzo Reale, Milan

1976 THE ARTIST AND THE   Israel Museum, Jerusalem
      PHOTOGRAPH

1977 EUROPE IN THE 70's   The Art Institute of Chicago;
1978   Hirshhorn Museum and Sculpture Garden, Washington;
                                  San Francisco Museum of Modern Art; Fort Worth Art
                                  Museum

1978 DOCUMENTA 6   Kassel

1978 38th BIENNALE   Venice

1981 16 BIENAL DE SÃO PAULO   São Paulo

1981 BRITISH SCULPTURE   Whitechapel Art Gallery, London
      IN THE TWENTIETH
      CENTURY

1982 DOCUMENTA 7   Kassel

1983 TRENDS IN POSTWAR   The Solomon R. Guggenheim Museum, New York
      AMERICAN AND EURO-
      PEAN ART

1984 PHOTGRAPHY IN   The National Museums of Art, Tokyo and Kyoto
      CONTEMPORARY ART

1984 THE BRITISH SHOW   Art Gallery of Western Australia; Art Gallery of New
                                 Soth Wales; Queensland Art Gallery

1984 DIALOG   Moderna Museet, Stockholm

1986 MATER DULCISSIMA   Chiesa dei Cavalieri di Malta, Syracuse

1987 FROM THE EUROPE   Stedelijk Museum, Amsterdam
      OF OLD

1987 BRITISH ART IN THE   Royal Academy of Arts, London; Staatsgalerie Stuttgart
      TWENTIETH CENTURY

1987 CURRENT AFFAIRS   Museum of Modern Art, Oxford; Budapest, Prague,
                                 Warsaw

1988 1988: THE WORLD OF ART   Milwaukee Art Museum
      TODAY

1988 COLLECTION   Centro de Arte Reina Sofia, Madrid
      SONNABEND

1989 BILDERSTREIT   Kölner Messe, Cologne

1990 GLASGOW'S GREAT BRIT-   Glasgow
      ISH ART EXHIBITION

1990 COLLECTION DU CAPC   capc Musée d'Art contemporain, Bordeaux
      MUSÉE

1991 METROPOLIS   Martin-Gropius-Bau, Berlin

BIBLIOGRAPHY
(Selected – listed chronologically)

Elk, Ger van   We would honestly like to say how happy we are to be sculptures, Museumjournaal, Nr. 5, Oct. 1969, 248–249

Tisdall, Caroline   Gilbert & George, The Guardian, 20 Nov. 1970

Pincus-Witten, R.   Gilbert & George, Artforum, Vol. 10, Dec. 1971, 78–79

Celant, Germano   Gilbert & George, Domus, Nr. 508, March 1972, 50–53

Seymour, Anne   An interview, The New Art Catalogue, London, Hayward Gallery/Arts, 1972, 92–95

Vaizey, Marina   Gilbert & George, The Financial Times, 30 Dec. 1972

Blotkamp, Carel   Gilbert & George: on cooperation on tradition, Album Amicorum, J. G. Van Gelder, The Hague, Nijhoff, 1973, 42–46

Amman, Jean-Chr.   Gilbert & George, Das Kunstwerk, Vol. 26, Jan. 1973, 35–44

Pluchart, F.   Gilbert & George, Human sculptures, Artitudes International, Nr. 3, Feb./March 1973, 16–17

Graf, U.   Zur Geschichte der lebenden Skulptur, Werk/Œuvre, Vol. 61, 1974, 219–225

Morris, Lynda   Gilbert & George, Studio International, Vol. 188, July/Aug. 1974, 49–50

Bologna, Ferdinando   Gilbert & George, Il Mattino, 13 May 1975

Ratcliff, Carter   The art and artlessness of Gilbert & George, Arts Magazine, Vol. 50, Jan. 1976, 54–57

Feaver, William   Mental images, The Observer, 30 May 1976

Haden-Guest, Anthony   The Red Sculpture, Paris Review, Winter 1976

Lucie-Smith, Edward   Ever so nice, Art & Artists, Vol. 11., March 1977, 27–29

Fuchs, Rudi   Gilbert & George, Art Monthly, Nr. 6, April 1977

Ratcliff, Carter   Down and out with Gilbert & George, Art in America, Vol. 66, May/June 1978, 92–93

Ratcliff, Carter   Gilbert & George and modern life, exh. cat. Gilbert & George 1968–1980, Van Abbemuseum, Eindhoven 1980

Celant, Germano   Gilbert & George, Books by artists, Toronto 1981, 100–101

Martin, Jean-H.   Un entretien avec Gilbert & George, supplement to exh. cat. Gilbert & George 1968–1980, Centre Georges Pompidou, Paris 1981

Wilson, Simon   Modern Fears, Burlington Magazine, Feb. 1981

Francis, Mark   Gilbert & George, An interview with Mark Francis, Whitechapel Art Gallery, London, 1 June 1981

Brown, Robert   The World of Gilbert & George, British Film Institute Monthly Film Bulletin, Dec. 1981, 257

Moravia, Alberto   Ma che belle statuine, L'Espresso, 1 Jan. 1982

Frey, Patrick   Gilbert & George in der Fremdheit ihrer Welt, Jahresbericht des Basler Kunstvereins, Kunsthalle Basle, Feb. 1982/83

Kaap, Gerald   Hunger and thirst, Zien Magazine Nr. 5, 1983

Van der Richardson, Brenda   No puzzle, just difficult truth, exh. cat. Gilbert & George Catalogue, Baltimore Museum of Art, 1984

Sewell, Brian   Two of a kind, Tatler, March 1984

Vaizey, Marina   To believe is to see, Sunday Times: 1 April 1984

Zevi, Adachiara   Life, a great sculpture, AEIOU Magazine, Nr. 10–11, July 1984

Brooks, R.   Shake hands with the devil, Artforum, Summer 1984

Csonka, Ariane   They'll give you something to talk about, The Miami Evening Times, 1 Oct. 1984

Mennekes, Friedhelm   Mythos und Bibel, Katholisches Bibelwerk GmbH, 1985

Hegewisch, Katharina   Helden der Zukunft, Frankfurter Allgemeine Zeitung, 30 Jan. 1985

Schwartz, Sanford   We are one, The New Yorker, 19 Aug. 1985

Davvetas, Demosthenes A conversation with Gilbert & George, exh. cat. Charcoal-on-paper sculptures Catalogue, Capc. Bordeaux, 1986

Jahn, Wolf   With us in the Nature, exh. cat. The Paintings Catalogue, Fruitmarket Gallery Edinburgh, 1986

Ratcliff, Carter   Gilbert & George: The Fabric of Their World, exh. cat. Gilbert & George, The Complete Pictures 1971–1985, Bordeaux, Basle, Brussels, Madrid, Munich, London, 1986/87

Codognato, Mario   Gilbert & George, L'Opera, L'Idee, Domus, May 1986

Albig, Jörg-Uwe   Die melancholischen Dandys, Art, June 1986

Jahn, Wolf   Neue Bilder eines neuen Lebens, Szene Hamburg, June 1985

Waibel, Jürgen   Das Duo ist unverschämt modern, Stuttgarter Nachrichten, 24 Oct. 1986

Brea, José Luis   El mundo de Gilbert & George, Sur Expres, Dec. 1986

Lucie-Smith, Edward   The Goyas of Spitalfields, Times, 1 Dec. 1986

Edward Jahn, Wolf   The human city, exh. cat. From the Europe of Old, Stedelijk Museum, Amsterdam 1987

Markowska, Anna und Wojciech   Gilbert & George, Przekrøj, Polen, March 1987

Several contributors   Collaboration with Gilbert & George, Parkett No. 14, Dec. 1987

Whitaker, Andrea   Gilbert & George. Die Zwillinge im Geiste, Pan Magazine, May 1988

Rosenblum, Robert   Gilbert & George: The Aids Pictures, Art in America, Nov. 1989, 153–155

Jahn, Wolf   Die Kunst von Gilbert & George, Munich, London, 1989

Hind, John   Feeling the World, Blitz, April 1989

Markowski, Wojciech   Gilbert & George, Osebe, O politike, O ideách Výtvarnýźivot, Poland, March 1990

Without author   exh. cat. Gilbert & George, Moscow, 1990

Rosenblum, Robert   exh. cat. Worlds and Windows by Gilbert & George, New York/London, 1990

Rozin, Alexander   Gilbert & George, USSR Creativity, April 1990

Mozgovoi, F.   Gilbert & George, Free Time in Moscow, 12 May 1990

Dany Lavich   Without Compliments, Soviet Culture, 12 May 1990

Han-Magomeford, V.   Red Leaves are Blossoming, Ezestiy. USSR (Information), 15 May 1990

Han-Magomeford, V.   This England ist not so Conservative, Moscow Comsomolez, 17 May 1990

M. L.   Are You Serious Sir, Moscow Conversationist, 19 May 1990

Bespalova, Helena   Art for All, Moscow News, 20 May, 1990

Michel Bourel   Commentaire de l'œuvre, capc Bordeaux collection, June 1990

Jahn, Wolf   The Paintings, capc Bordeaux collection, June 1990

Camus, Renaud   Natura Naturata, capc Bordeaux collection, June 1990

Troy   Doubles all round. The Art of Gilbert & George, Vada, Oct. 1990

Farson, Daniel   Victims of the British desease, Mail on Sunday, 21 Oct. 1990
Bespalova, Helena   Gilbert & George, Decorative Arts USSR, Nov. 1990
Mikheyev, Mikhail   Fantastic! Terrible! Artscribe, Nov./Dec. 1990

PHOTOGRAPHY CREDITS

P. 16, Uwe Steffen: *Das Mysterium von Tod und Wiedergeburt,* Göttingen 1963.

P. 17, left: Nikos v. Georgiades: *Mistra,* Athens 1971; right: *Christenfreude in Lied und Bild,* Leipzig, in commision to Georg Wigand, 1855.

P. 19, see page 16.

P. 21, from left to right, from the top to the bottom: 1. Bodhisattva Jizô, Japan, 13th–14th century (Roger Goepper: *Kunst und Kunsthandwerk Ostasiens,* Munich 1968); 2. St. George, about 1475 (The Metropolitan Museum of Art, New York); 3. Statue from the tomb of Kaaper the priest (Egypt), 5th Dynasty (Egyptian Museum, Cairo); 4. Emperor Claudius, bronze cast from Herkulaneum (Museo Archeologico Nazionale, Naples); 5. female Kazike from the Quimbaya-culture, Columbia, 4th–7th century (Museum für Völkerkunde, Berlin); 6. The Royal Bodyguard of Darius the Great, Persepolis (Sylvia A. Matheson: *Persia: an archaelogical guide,* London 1972); 7. Zôchô-ten, king of the southern heaven, Japan, 8th century (see 1.).

P. 22, from left to right, from the top to the bottom: 1. Indian gate-kepper (Louis Fréderic: *Indien, Tempel und Skulpturen,* Zurich/Stuttgart, 1959); 2. Figure on the roof of a meeting-house, New Zealand [Enrico Guidoni (ed.): *Architektur der primitiven Kulturen,* Milan 1975, Stuttgart 1976]; 3. The god of corn of the Monte Albán-culture, Mexico (Museum für Völkerkunde, Berlin); 4. Emperor Leopoldus Primus, figure standing on the stern of a Hamburg convoyship, 1668–1705 (Museum für Hamburgische Geschichte); 5. Holder of the stabbing "Kris", Bali, 19th century (Museum für Völkerkunde, Berlin); 6. Sculpture of an ancestor of the Namatanai (Pacific) [Herbert Tischner: *Dokumente verschollener Südseekulturen,* Nuremberg, 1981]; 7. Warrior form the Marquesas-Islands (from: G.H. v. Langsdorffs Reise um die Welt 1803–05, in: *The Ring of Fire, Polynesian Art,* New York, 1967, vol. 1); 8. Chief's stool from Bekom, Kamerun (Museum für Völkerkunde, Berlin); 9. Sun God of North American Indians (Bildarchiv Foto Marburg); 10. Virgin in the chapel Saint-Jean de l'Ouradou, beginning of 15th century (Jacqueline Boccador: *Statuaire Médiévale en France de 1400 á 1530,* vol. I); 11. St. James by Gil de Siloe, Burgos, Spain, 1489–93 (The Metropolitan Museum of Art); 12. Statue of the god Visnu, Thailand, 7th century (National Museum Bangkok); 13. The goddess Athena, marble copy of an original bronze, 5th century B.C. (Museo Archeologico Nazionale, Naples).

P. 39, exh. cat.: *Prag um 1600,* Essen 1988.

P. 40, Albert Speer: *Architektur, Arbeiten 1933–1942,* Frankfurt/Main 1978.

P. 42, Dietrich Mühlberg (ed.): *Proletariat, Kultur und Lebensweise im 19. Jhdt.,* Vienna, Cologne, Graz, 1986.

P. 45, left: see page 22, 2.

P. 47, from left to right, top: 1. Karl Loeffler: *Schwäbische Buchmalerei in romanischer Zeit,* Augsburg 1928; 2. Pergamon Museum, Berlin; bottom: 3. Bildarchiv Foto Marburg; 4. Marcel Pobé and Jean Roubier: *Das gotische Frankreich,* Vienna/Munich 1960.

P. 48, from left to right, top: 1. Michael W. Meister (ed.): *Encyclopedia of Indian Temple Architecture,* Pennsylvania, 1986, Vol. 1, Plates 2; 2. *Bild der Völker,* die Brockhaus Völkerkunde, vol. 6, Wiesbaden, 1974; bottom: 3. The Metropolitan Museum of Art; 4. see page 22, 2.

P. 49, from left to right, top: 1. Louis Fréderic: *Südostasien – Tempel und Skulpturen,* Essen, 1968; 2. Bildarchiv Foto Marburg; bottom: 3. exh. cat. *In the Image of Man,* London. 1982; 4. Mario Bussagli: *Architektur des Orients,* Milan 1973, Stuttgart, 1975.

P. 50, see page 49. 4.
P. 53, see page 42.